Stories We Tell Ourselves

sightline books

The Iowa Series in Literary Nonfiction

Patricia Hampl & Carl H. Klaus, series editors

Michelle Herman
Stories We Tell Ourselves
"Dream Life" and "Seeing Things"

University of Iowa Press   Iowa City

University of Iowa Press, Iowa City 52242
Copyright © 2013 by Michelle Herman
www.uiowapress.org
Printed in the United States of America
Text design by Richard Hendel

The University of Iowa Press is a member of
Green Press Initiative and is committed to preserving
natural resources.
Printed on acid-free paper

ISBN-13: 978-1-60938-153-0
ISBN-10: 1-60938-153-X
LCCN: 2012945880

FOR GRACE,

AND FOR MY MOTHER.

AND THIS ONE'S FOR KATHY, TOO.

. . . remember most of all
to be enthusiastic over the night,
not only for the sense of wonder
it alone has to offer, but also

because it needs our love. With large sad eyes
its delectable creatures look up and beg
us dumbly to ask them to follow . . .

W. H. AUDEN
In Memory of Sigmund Freud

Contents

Acknowledgments

I am very grateful to Bret Lott, Dave Blum, Catherine Cocks, Charlotte Wright, and Kris Bjork; to my stalwart friend and agent, Marian B.S. Young; to the Ohio Arts Council; and to my father and my brother, Morton Herman and Scott Herman, for the kind of support that money can't buy *and* the kind it can.

Portions of this book appeared, in different forms, in *The Southern Review* and as a Kindle Single.

Dream Life

1

All day today I have been feeling melancholy and nostalgic, teary-eyed and loving toward all creatures great and small (from husband to cockatiel). Whereas yesterday all day I was irritable and angry—scolding the bird for chirping, yanking the dog when she didn't move along fast enough to suit me, snapping at the husband when he asked if there was anything for dinner. And nothing happened between yesterday and today to change my mood—nothing except for a night's sleep, and a dream from which I woke up cured of all bad feeling.

There is something of the chicken-or-the-egg about this. Was it the dream that sweetened my disposition—a gift from the dream gods? Or was it simply that the bad day I'd had was over, and I was ready to start fresh (with a new, improved attitude) and thus inclined to view the dream—which was not at all on the face of it a "good dream"—tenderly, just as I have viewed and treated everything and everyone around me all day long today?

The dream was about my grandmother, as my dreams so often are, though it's been fifteen years now since her death. Sometimes in my dreams she is very old—as old as she got to be in real life—and sometimes she's in her sixties or seventies, as she was in my childhood and youth, but even in those dreams I am almost always my present middle aged self, and aware that she is much younger than she should be.

She was fifty-seven when I was born, and ninety-five when she died. Until last night I had never dreamed her younger or older than I'd known her in real life. But in last night's dream she was ancient—as old as she would be if she were still alive today. And she was *tiny*, not much more than a handful of bones. She couldn't speak; she could hardly move. She was living in the terrible apartment in East Flatbush where she lived in real life in the early 1990s, the place where she was living when she died—the place in *which* she died, sitting in the chair in the living room where she sat all day, every day, that final year of her life.

I should mention that neither she nor I ever managed to think of this apartment as her home. It was in a cheerless little building, part of a housing project of twenty identically cheerless buildings, in a grimly rundown (and, worse—for her, for me—unfamiliar) neighborhood, and it was even smaller than the small apartment in Brighton Beach where she'd lived for over half a century. Each time I went to see her in her "new" apartment, it struck me that she still hadn't truly moved in. No one had had the heart, I suppose, to sort through her things before the move, and afterward there seemed to be no place to put them all. In every corner there were cardboard boxes and plastic and paper grocery bags and shopping bags imprinted with the names of stores that had gone out of business years ago, all of them stuffed full of papers, cards, photographs, knitted and crocheted things she'd made tucked into still more plastic bags from Speedway and John's Bargain Store, hats my grandfather had made during his years at the hat factory, leftover scraps of fabric, balls of yarn and pillow stuffing and jars of buttons, squares of folded-up, used giftwrap and tinfoil, and all kinds of assorted *junk*. There wasn't room for all her furniture in the new apartment, either, but it had all come with her anyway, and there was furniture everywhere, positioned at odd angles.

She hadn't wanted to move. *I* hadn't wanted her to move. She'd been living alone since my grandfather's death, in 1982, and for a long time that had been all right, or mostly all right. At the beginning I visited once a week and so did my mother, and we both called her every day. But in the autumn of 1984 I moved away, for graduate school in Iowa, and by 1988 I was living in Ohio, where I'd found a teaching job. My mother kept making weekly trips from Manhattan; my Uncle Aaron, the eldest of my grandmother's children and the only one who still lived in Brooklyn, stopped in for at least a few minutes every few days. But by the late 1980s, Aaron was in his seventies; his wife, Aunt Shirley, had died, and he wasn't altogether well himself. And so just as my grandmother, now past ninety, began to require more frequent check-ins, Aaron told us that he was finding it increasingly difficult to make the trip so often from his place to hers—a distance of less than six miles that felt like more than that to all of us, and not just because there wasn't a good direct driving route between the two neighborhoods.

Brighton Beach was where my grandmother had raised three of her four children. It was where she and my grandfather had landed safely, like so many other Eastern European Jews, after escaping first from the Lower East Side, their initial stop in the U.S., and then Borough Park, their second (where they'd lingered for some time—until Aaron was grown, and my mother, the baby, was four years old). Brighton Beach was where the old people, most of them born at the turn of the century, all of them born on the other side of the ocean, dragged folding chairs downstairs and set them up along the wrought iron fence around the building, where they sat and gossiped all day in a mixture of Yiddish and English. "How's Grandma?" they called to me when I visited, when she became too frail to join them (not that she admitted this; what she said was that she couldn't bear the gossiping anymore. "Who needs it?" she told me. "Better to sit in the house and mind my own business").

I'd lived in that building myself, just down the hall from my grandparents, until I was three and my mother was pregnant with my brother. The old people had known me all my life. Their *children* had known me all my life. The building was as close to a homeplace (something I knew about only from novels) as it was possible for me to have.

But there was nothing for it. When an apartment became available in the building Aaron had lived in nearly as long as his mother had lived in hers—the place where he and Shirley had raised *their* children, now long grown and scattered, with children of their own—my grandmother was moved in to it.

Aaron stopped by to see her in the new apartment at least once every day. My mother kept up her weekly visits and called daily. I called nearly every day, too, from five hundred miles away (in those days when long distance calls were still something of a luxury, when one waited until after 5:00 PM to place a call—or, better still, after 11:00). My brother, who had just moved back to the East Coast from Chicago, visited as often as he could; my Uncles Isaac and David, both of whom, like my brother, lived in New Jersey, called and dropped in, too, if inconsistently, and once in a great while one of my cousins turned up. But it wasn't long before visits and phone calls, no matter how many or from whom or how long they lasted, weren't sufficient. Full-time "home health workers" were engaged, at first to make sure Grandma was eating (for she had reached the point at which the only thing that had "any taste," she said, was bread sprinkled with Tabasco sauce, and some days she wouldn't even want "to be bothered" with that: "I'm not hungry anyway. Why should I go to so much trouble?") and to remind her to take her various pills. Soon it was to bathe her and dress her, too, and to take her to the bathroom in the middle of the night. And finally it was to keep an eye on her every minute of every day.

It was one of these home health workers who was with her on the day she died. She had been dozing on and off in her chair all day, and she had opened her eyes and cleared her throat and asked for something to drink. Her helper went to the kitchen to get her a glass of water, and when she returned with it, my grandmother was gone.

But in my dream, none of this had happened—none of it except the move from Brighton Beach to East Flatbush. In my dream, many years had passed, and in all that time my grandmother had been alone in the apartment. She was so tiny and silent and immobile because she hadn't eaten anything in all those years. But now—just as the dream began—something was happening, some kind of celebration. My whole family had gathered around her in that gloomy, overstuffed apartment, and as the days passed, she grew visibly more robust. By the end of the celebration, as everyone prepared to leave, calling out goodbyes, gathering up coats and tinfoil-wrapped leftovers, she was young and strong again. And she was *beautiful*. She looked like a movie star. She was slim and glamorous, with a fifties hourglass figure and long blond curls, dressed to the nines, in high heels. She might even have been wearing a mink stole. She looked nothing like herself at any stage of her real life, the life in which she had married at seventeen and begun a career of housework and worry. The few photographs that exist of her as a girl, newly arrived in the States at fifteen, show her to be handsome and stern and solid-looking, a little bit stout, with her long, unruly, dark brown hair—hair just like mine, she always told me—bound up in a bun.

It was understood, the way things are understood in dreams, that *not being alone* was what had "cured" her. And so it was clear to me what had to be done. I was going to take her home with me to Ohio, to make sure that she would never have to be alone again.

In real life, I had actually tried to do that. When I bought a house in Columbus after my first year of teaching, it was one with a room in it that was earmarked for her, and I set about trying to persuade her to come live in it. I was *determined* to persuade her, but I got nowhere. She insisted that it was impossible for her to move in with me: she couldn't be so far away from "the children." We discussed this, debated it — argued about it — for months. And my dream acknowledged this (that I had tried and failed, years ago), but in the dream I squared my shoulders, ready to try again. I had logic on my side this time, I told myself, as I followed my glamour-girl grandmother around her gloomy little apartment, making my case. Ohio would be easier now, I argued, since there were only two, not four, of her children to be far away *from*. What I meant was that only two were alive — Aaron and my mother. (But this was dream-logic. In real life, Aaron is long gone. In the dream, it was my mother's two other brothers, both of whom *are* still living — they are in their eighties now, the elder of them nearly as frail as my grandmother was toward the end of her life — who were gone, and Aaron still alive.) Aaron and my mother would visit her in Ohio, I promised. They would be *happy* if she came with me. Even in the dream I was not sure this was true, but I said it as if I were.

In my dream I did not note, as I did once I woke up, that it was the children my grandmother could count on — her eldest and her youngest — who were alive, that the absence of the other two would make very little difference in her day-to-day life. My grandmother didn't say it either, just as she would never have said it in real life. In real life, she had often expressed favoritism (which had infuriated my father and brother; my mother claimed it didn't bother her) toward her youngest son, Davey — the one who paid her the least attention, the one who was selfish and breezy and uninvolved (and who, in real life, moved to California before her death and cut off contact with all of us, after a dispute that only appeared to be about money. There was no money, but that has never stopped families in all sorts of other kinds of trouble from arguing over it).

It didn't matter, anyway — what I said or did not say — because my grandmother wasn't having any of it. "It's no good," she kept interrupting me to say. "*This* is where I live."

But it wasn't, I told her. "This isn't home. You don't even like it here."

"It's less far," she told me. "I can't go so far."

I began to panic as I watched one after another of her guests kiss her and walk out the door. I knew that once she was left alone, she would lose every bit of ground she'd gained. She would grow old again, and soon it would all be over—this time for good. And I had to *go*. It seemed that I was on a schedule; I didn't have much time. I stood there anxiously telling myself that there must be something I could do, something I could say—I just had to *think* (surely I could think of something!)—as the curtain fell on the dream, as I woke up in tears, thinking, *I'm not going anywhere without you.*

In my waking life—my "real life"—there was good reason for me to have been in a bad mood yesterday. The night before, my daughter had come home from a week at camp. I had missed her and was delighted to see her; *she*, however, was not happy to be home. When she deigned to speak to me at all, it was tersely, crossly, sarcastically.

My daughter is fifteen, and so one might imagine that all of the above should go without saying.

But in truth it does not. My daughter and I are close—unusually close (unnaturally close, some would say), just as my grandmother and I were. We are closer, in fact, than my grandmother and I were, because Grace and I have lived together all of Grace's life, and because times have changed (there were subjects I would not have dared to broach with my grandmother, for fear of shocking her; I've made sure that Grace has no such qualms), and because Grace and I have similar temperaments and are interested in many of the same things, while my grandmother and I had to reach across great barriers of temperament and experience and affinities as we made our way toward each other in friendship—although we had in common, it occurs to me now, one crucial experience: as children we had both felt rejected by our mothers. Whereas my daughter, unlike my grandmother and me—and unlike my own mother—has never felt neglected or abandoned. (On the contrary, she has sometimes felt—has sometimes been—*over*mothered.)

I was not only surprised and wounded by Grace's surliness and dismissiveness—I also felt foolish. Worse than foolish: I felt pathetic, obsolete. I had outlived my usefulness and I hadn't even known it—that was how I felt.

And this week at camp, a singing camp at the university where I teach, where she stayed in a dorm and ate bad cafeteria food (or so she had reported gleefully *last* summer, her first at "Harmony Camp"—her first away at *any* camp—from which she'd come home full of news and delighted to see her family, her room, her dog, her bird), had served as a preview of coming attractions. In just three years, I'd reflected as I pulled up at her dorm a week ago (and she jumped out, calling, "You don't have to come in this year—I know where to go"), I'd be dropping her off for her freshman year on a college campus, no doubt one considerably farther away. When she comes home then—and forever after—it will be for visits only. And only as frequently or infrequently as she chooses.

I had worked myself up into a panic by bedtime. And with the panic came self-castigation and shame. What did I want, after all, I asked myself angrily: to lock her in a tower so that I might call up, "Let down your hair" like old Mother Gothel, the witch determined to keep teenage Rapunzel all to herself?

Here is the puzzle—one of the many puzzles—of dreaming:

It's not as if I didn't *know*, before I went to sleep and dreamed, that my daughter's growing up was—is—inevitable. Or didn't know how much I want to keep her near me . . . or that in some ways she will always *be* near me. (How near to me, after all, my grandmother always was, even when we were hundreds of miles apart. How near to me she still is, even fifteen years after her death. *Fifteen!* It is only as I write this that I stop to think about it: that Grace's years on earth match the years my grandmother has been gone from it.)

It's not as if I didn't know that I am fearful, now that I have passed fifty, of growing old myself. Of growing old, of death. It's not as if I haven't thought, *I am nearer now to death than not.*

It's not as if I didn't know that I have felt neglected, deprived (*starved*) in some way all my life.

And it's not as if I didn't know that my daughter's presence—her existence—has done much to ease my chronic loneliness; it's not as if I didn't remember that the very day she was born I believed myself to be "cured" of it (that was the word I used, although when I said it aloud—to my husband, my mother, my friends—I pretended I was joking), or that even before her birth, all the while I was pregnant with her, I marveled over how *un*lonely I felt. It's not even as if I'd forgotten that it was while I was pregnant with Grace that my grandmother began to fail, that I flew home to see her in the hospital when I was only a few weeks along—that before I'd even told my parents, I whispered the news to her, and that she put her hand on my still-flat belly and beamed at me, and then somehow rallied one more time. It's not as if I *could* forget that she stayed alive just long enough to see the baby once—although by then, the next time I visited, when Grace was three months old, her mind was slipping away, and when I knelt beside her in that apartment I hated and put my daughter into her arms, she asked me, "Whose baby is this? Who has brought a baby to me?"

But I wasn't thinking about any of this yesterday. I wasn't thinking about anything except how wretched I felt. I didn't even linger on the immediate *cause* of my wretchedness. That is, I was aware that Grace's homecoming had been a disappointment, and I was aware that I was miserable, but I wasn't thinking about the connection between the two.

And then I went to sleep and dreamed.

Deprivation, guilt, shame, loneliness, abandonment, neglect, loss, home, isolation, the inexorable passage of time, impossible choices, mothers and children, youth and age, old age and death—everything turned up in last night's dream, repackaged in a narrative that delivered an arrow to my heart (*another* arrow to my heart). *You see how it is? This is how it is.*

I'm not going anywhere without you.

You'd think such a dream would have left me feeling *worse* than I'd been feeling when I went to bed. You'd think I would have woken up distraught, or frightened—or angry (*Why won't she do as I ask? Why won't she come with me?*) or resigned, grief-stricken, depressed.

It's true that I was sad when I first woke from the dream. Sad, and shaken. And—this struck me before I was fully awake—*chastened.* But I also felt (and this was the word I used in my mind, just as it was the word I had used during my pregnancy—just as it was the word

I had used in the dream, to describe my grandmother's miraculous transformation) *cured.*

I want to be clear. I don't mean to say that my dream "taught me a lesson," that the narrative spun out by my unconscious mind was designed (by my own unconscious mind) as a parable. What I do mean is that the dream coaxed me into making connections that I didn't—couldn't—make while I was awake (awake and feeling so sorry for myself): that the dream reminded me of all the things I knew, patiently spelling out for me the connections between the things I knew and the things I was feeling, and pointing out the things I was feeling now that I'd felt before. The dream didn't *fix* anything, but it helped me make peace with how I felt—just as I'd had to make peace (uneasy and inconstant as it was) with my grandmother's refusal, in real life, to spend what was left of her life with me, so that she wouldn't have to be alone.

"*Alone?*" my grandmother would say when I told her that—told her how I hated for her to be alone, and how she didn't have to be. "*Ha*"—she would bark out a little laugh—"I am always alone." By which I thought she meant, "I would be alone anyway, even if I were to come live with you. *Svet gornisht helfen*—it wouldn't help." I thought she was telling me, "In my heart, I am, and forever will be, alone."

But perhaps she meant only, "I am *accustomed* to being alone. It's nothing to me now," or even, "I have come to like being alone." (Perhaps that syllable of laughter meant, "How silly of you not to understand this." Perhaps it made her bitter that I—even I!—did not understand.)

Why did I never *ask* her? Why did I only argue with her? "You don't *have* to be alone," I told her—told her the same thing again and again—and provided a list of reasons (the same reasons again and again) that she should agree to move five hundred miles away from everything and everyone she knew except me. And then I'd hang up the phone feeling rebuffed, dismissed, irrelevant, frustrated, guilty. I should have tried harder, I'd tell myself. She isn't being reasonable. Certainly she's not acting in her own best interests. If only she'd listen!

I'm the one who knows what's best for her. I'm the only one.

2

I f I were not the sort of person who takes dreams seriously, it would not even have crossed my mind that my dream had been curative (if I even remembered it—if I even woke up knowing that I'd *had* a dream). But I have been paying close attention to my dreams all my life. I can't recall a time when I did not wake from a dream and think, *Now, what does* that *mean?*

As it was, I didn't have to think very hard about last night's dream for it to "work." The dream itself did everything, making use of what had been on my mind all day that I had been doing my best not to think about even as it also made use of what was well beneath the surface of my mind. The dream reminded me of what my feelings reminded me of, making plain the links between what I was experiencing in my waking, present-day, "real" life and what was alive only in my mind—in my memory, in my sense of myself. Thus a dream that was rooted in how deeply unhappy I had been all day had yanked from the ground *of* the day all of that unhappiness and cooked it overnight—set it on the heat of sleep, stirred it, left it simmering—and managed to produce a sort of healing broth.

It's no wonder that ancient cultures considered dreams to be gifts from the gods.

It was Aristotle who first proposed that dreaming was the mind's activity during sleep. Before him (and long after, too—for in his thinking about the mind, as in his thinking about ethics, aesthetics, politics, zoology, and formal logic, he was centuries ahead of his time), dreaming was considered to be a matter of metaphysics, portents, and secret messages from the spirit world.

The idea of *repressed* thoughts showing up in dreams wasn't formulated until over twenty-two hundred years after Aristotle. This was the contribution of "W. Robert," a nineteenth-century dream theorist whose idea was cited by Freud in *The Interpretation of Dreams* (1900). Robert's notion was that dreams were the manifestations of thoughts "stifled at birth" (a crackpot idea, reported soberly by Freud). It was Freud himself, of course, who offered the theory that emotions buried in the unconscious mind will turn up in disguise in our dreams, that the fragments we remember of these dreams can be interpreted, and that these interpretations can help us uncover such buried feelings.

Freud considered dreams to be the "royal road to the unconscious." But dream narratives have been contemplated and interpreted by dreamers at least as far back as we have evidence of human beings contemplating anything at all. Dream content *begs* for interpretation. The early Greeks used dreams for medical diagnosis; the Romans established temples dedicated to Aesculapius, the god of medicine, in which people would bathe, fast, perform rituals, and then sleep, hoping to be granted a healing dream. Dream interpretation is mentioned in Homer; the Greek orator and statesman Demosthenes, in the fourth century B.C.E., claimed to have received messages from the gods in his sleep; Artemidorus (second century C.E.) was a professional dream-diviner, telling people's fortunes based on their dreams.

Ever since Freud, however, we have made use of dreams for what the contemporary "sleep and dream scientist" J. Allan Hobson derisively calls "psychological divinations."

To Hobson, a psychiatrist, dream content is meaningless — it's "cognitive trash." Dreaming is like psychosis, he says, for in our dreams, places and even people change without reason or warning; there are sudden inexplicable time shifts that seem to make perfect sense. Are these not some of the very cognitive deficits that characterize psychosis? Night after night, we tell ourselves lies about ourselves in our dreams — and in our dreams we are certain that these lies are true; night after night, things happen that in our right minds we would know were impossible.

In the dream I had last night (Hobson might point out), I was convinced that people who are dead are actually alive — something I would never be confused about in my waking life — and an event was taking place, a family gathering in my grandmother's "new" apartment, that never happened in real life (and yet I had no doubt that it *was* happening). And although my grandmother, by the end of the dream, looked like someone else entirely, I knew it was she—it never occurred to me to question this.

Hobson suggests that there is a simple explanation for the way "we go mad each night" (as he puts it). The psychosis we experience during sleep is the result, he says, of altered brain chemistry: changes in the levels of three chemicals in the brain, the hormones norepinephrine (or noradrenaline), serotonin, and acetylcholine. When we sleep, the levels of the first two hormones go down, and the third goes up. These changes, Hobson says, represent a kind of "balancing act." The neurons in the brainstem that produce norepinephrine and serotonin—neurotransmitters that are essential for various mental activities we engage in while awake (orienting ourselves, remembering things, paying attention, concentrating, having insights, and so on)—become desensitized after we have been awake for too long, so we have to "turn them off for a while" and give them a rest. Why we would also dramatically increase the production of acetylcholine—the "stuff [that] drives you nuts," as Hobson describes it—to help achieve this "balance" is more puzzling to him, but its effects, he says, are clear: "Your visual and emotional centers are being bombarded [by acetylcholine]. You are basically having a modified seizure."

Actually, since Hobson, as well as other contemporary scientists who study sleep and dreaming, also believes that the purpose of sleep is to refresh our skills (skills such as when to approach, when to mate, when to be afraid, and when to run for cover), and that the maintenance of the "emotional systems" of the brain (including terror and anxiety, which are among the most common emotions in our dreams) is what ensures our survival, the chemical-induced craziness Hobson describes may *be*—at least in Hobson's account of the way our minds work—the function of dreaming. If our dreams are intended to drive us temporarily "nuts" so that we can practice reacting to extreme situations and emotions (something like a fire drill—or the atomic bomb drills we had at school when I was growing up), then an acetylcholine spike would be as essential for our overall well-being as the nightly shutting off of the brain chemicals that help us keep our wits about us.

To today's dream researchers, then, dreaming is thus explicable as something like hiding under our desks, pretending that there has been a nuclear attack, to make sure we're ready when the attack comes in real life.

But here is what I wonder: if dream narratives are no more than a snatching-up of random bits of our day's activities, fragments of memories, and assorted acetylcholine-driven hallucinations, gathered together in the service of keeping us fit to react to real-life crises and decisions, why do they have the effect on us that they do? Why are they so *personal*? And why is it that Hobson himself, like his mentor, Michel Jouvet—both of whom argue that there *is* no interpreting dreams, that even "so-called free association" (as they regularly refer to it) is worthless when it comes to dreams—cannot resist offering his own associations when he describes dreams *he* has had? Why has he kept a dream notebook for four decades?

The idea that our dreams are messengers, bringing us the news from our hidden selves, is a stubborn one. Once it has occurred to you, it seems impossible to dislodge the notion.

And why *should* you dislodge it?

Among "the messages" the dream I had last night brought me out of the soup of my unconscious was acceptance of the inevitable, however troubling, and a reminder (not a gentle one, for I *needed* an ungentle one) of the way celebration and sorrow seem always to be tangled together. These are excellent messages: why would I want to send them back unread?

(And apparently, even Hobson, who has written sternly about the importance of rejecting any dream interpretation that isn't "tied to physiology" in a straightforward way, can't bring himself to refuse the "messages" of his dreams: in his dream journal, he unselfconsciously and unironically writes at length about what his dreams suggest to him.)

It is not so surprising, really, that my sleeping mind should have stirred up my grief over my grandmother and my own dread of being left alone—and the way I had missed Grace for the short time she had been gone, and my belief that only *I* stood between my grandmother and her loneliness (and her death) and my fear that it is only Grace who stands between me and mine—not to mention all the other flotsam and jetsam of emotion and fact that turned up in my dream: the party, which brings to mind the fiftieth birthday celebration

I made for myself, gathering together nearly everyone who has ever been important to me, in an effort (of which I was quite conscious) to turn something I dreaded into an occasion for joy; the food the visiting relatives were carrying off—just as I always carried away tinfoil-wrapped packages of food after visits to my grandmother in the years before my grandfather's death, when she was still cooking—just as I sent guests home from my birthday party with foil-wrapped leftover lamb chops and roasted vegetables and loaves of artisanal bread; the apartment in which my grandmother spent the last years of her life, and which I so hated.

But what is miraculous to me is that the process, the labor, of folding all of this together was done while I *slept*. That while I slept, my mind was hard at work to help me see what I could not see while I was awake. That our minds have the capacity to do this for us every night.

Freud spoke of the "three great humiliations" in human history: Galileo's confirming what Copernicus had theorized—that the earth was not in fact at the center of the universe; Darwin's breaking the news to us of our ancestry; and Freud's informing us that we were not, as we had so stubbornly imagined, in control of our own minds.

What Freud offered along with this "humiliation," however, was a series of ideas about how we might gain access to the mysteries of our minds. Slips of the tongue, neurotic symptoms, and dreams could be examined closely and provide information that would close the gap between the conscious and unconscious mind. That he made a further argument about dreams—that they represent wish fulfillments, and that those wishes are the result of repressed sexual desire (and that it is the anxiety associated with these desires that creates nightmares)—is perhaps the single biggest obstacle to embracing Freudian theory today. But however dubiously one regards his notions about sex and desire, one cannot credit him *enough* for the stride forward he made in how we are able to think about the way our minds work.

Indeed, to dismiss dream content, to insist that dreams are physiological events that tell us virtually nothing about what resides in our (so-called) unconscious minds, flies in the face of what most of us *instinctively* feel: that our dreams have meaning, and can be traced (if not reflexively and immediately, then with a little patience, and with the help of those neurotransmitters that flow freely again once we are awake) to feelings, experiences—even ideas—that are rooted in our "real" lives.

A study conducted recently by two psychologists—Carey Morewedge from Carnegie Mellon and Michael Norton from Harvard—on the importance their subjects placed on dreams, suggests that few people believe "in modern theories that dreaming is simply the brain's response to random impulses, or that it's a mechanism for sorting and discarding information." The vast majority of their respondents, in all three countries in which the researchers conducted interviews—India, South Korea, and the United States—assumed that their dreams were telling them something they wouldn't have known otherwise, and that what they were being told, whether they understood it or not, was important.

This sense of "importance," the notion that a dream not only brings a message but that its message is not to be taken lightly, has long been with us. Ancient Egyptians believed that the gods revealed themselves in dreams specifically to give advice, to issue warnings or demands, or to make prophecies. Roman military leaders hired dream interpreters—haruspices—to travel with their armies, so that messages from the gods about battles to come could be quickly decoded, and Augustus himself is said to have benefited from a premonitory dream that saved his life in the battle of Philippi in 42 B.C.E. against the murderers of Julius Caesar. During Augustus's reign as Emperor (27 B.C.E. to 14 C.E.), anyone who dreamed about the Roman state was required to declare it publicly.

The Hebrew Bible, which predates the second century B.C.E. (and parts may date back to the seventh century B.C.E.), is full of references to significant dreams. Some scholars believe that dreaming was a source of inspiration and even divine guidance during the founding of Judaism. But even in the sixteenth century C.E., Solomon Almoli, a rabbi, physician, writer, and Hebrew grammarian, wrote in his *Interpretation of Dreams* that we were not to question God's power to introduce portents to us while we slept (these portents were so much more readily available to us in our sleep than while we were awake, he said, because in sleep "our physical energies are weakened and the mental strengthened").

How were such messages given to us? One notion firmly held by numerous cultures was that while the body slept, the soul left its corporeal prison, free to wander and report back later. In native North American culture, the dreaming soul—the aspect of the self that travels in visions—could regularly contact the dream spirit and receive instructions. Dreams were considered by many native American groups to be the most reliable way to communicate with spiritual powers; thus, dreams were the fundamental basis of religious knowledge. Advanced dreamers would become religious specialists, available to interpret dreams in order to diagnose illness, foretell the death or the return to health of the sick, and predict the outcome of expeditions in hunting and warfare. Among the Choctaws, Creeks, and Cherokees, there were dreamers who—according to Lee Irwin, Chair of Religious Studies at the College of Charleston, and the author of *The Dream Seekers: Native American Visionary Traditions of the Great Plains*—"could travel to a village of the dead and there converse with their former relatives."

When I converse with my dead relatives in dreams, I don't ever imagine—not even in my sleep—that they are speaking to me from beyond the grave. When I wake up, I am certain not only that I have conjured them from memory and longing, but that I've summoned them on this particular night for a particular reason. Of course, I am as much a product of my culture(s)—modernist, psychoanalytical, secularly Jewish, and literary, among others—as dreamers in other cultures and at other times have been of theirs. In other words, it seems plain to me that we believe about our dreams what we *must* believe, in the context of everything else we believe in. (Thus Hobson et al., I suppose it's fair to say, do their best to believe about dreams what their culture of "science" insists upon.)

But even a believer needn't (shouldn't?) take her faith for granted. Even a believer may be astonished—awestruck—by the way dreams work, by what a good job they do of sweeping up the raw material of one's waking life in order to bring that news from the unconscious. Consider how the dream I had last night, for example, collected every bad feeling of the day, including some that had been pretty well buried (I'll die without her; this place isn't even *home* without her), reached for metaphors from other parts of my experience, and made it clear to me that there was continuity between them. And it didn't even reach for *difficult* metaphors, didn't offer up a complicated, hard-to-follow continuity. My dream, it seems to me, did a remarkable job of communicating exactly what needed to be communicated: there was no showing off, no purposeful obscurity.

I like that in a dream. It impresses me (after all, I know how hard it is to express the mysterious without *being* mysterious, to be artful yet clear—and still subtle enough to be interesting; I know that choosing just the right details—the necessary details—only *looks* easy). It pleases me, too, now that I am wide awake and thinking clearly, to take note of how everything about the relationship between what I dreamed and what I was experiencing in my waking life is so *straight-forward*; it leaves me feeling that I have a healthy, happy relationship with my own unconscious—which, I suspect, is another reason I felt so much better in the morning. I am always pleased to find that I am not keeping too many secrets from myself.

But there were other reasons the dream cheered me up, I'm sure. Not the least of which was that I'd had the chance to see my grand-mother again.

Thanks to my dream, on and off all day today I have been thinking about her. It is as if my dream had whispered, *Remember*. Except for a brief period when I was (wait for it) the age my daughter is now, and again at the end of her life, when she was nearly as frail as she appeared at the beginning of last night's dream and was lost to me (lost to us all, lost to herself), my grandmother was my best friend. For years, we talked on the phone every day; when I was in my twenties, we sometimes talked for hours after my grandfather went to sleep. She never tired of complaining about his "bad habits": "First he falls asleep at seven o'clock in front of the television, in the chair. And I say, 'Go to bed!' So he gets up and he goes to lie down on the couch. More television, and again he falls asleep. So I shake him awake—by now it's already nine o'clock—and I make him go to bed. Why can't he go to bed to begin with?" And I never tired of saying, "Let him be. What difference does it make? This is how he likes it."

But we didn't talk only about my grandfather and his habits—his bedtime routine; his insistence on going out to do the shopping even though, if he would just wait patiently, Aaron would stop by in a few days and do it for them; the way he followed her around the apartment, "bothering" her. We talked about everything. We were fonder of each other, I think, than either of us were of anyone else, and we trusted each other without reservation. One does not have many such relationships in a lifetime. I have never had another, I suppose—except for the one I have with Grace, and it's no surprise that on the rare days when Grace and I are not the close companions we have been steadily for the last fifteen years, my grandmother should come back to me in a dream.

When I was Grace's age, I was nothing like her. *She* is nearly always kind, grateful for everything she has, compassionate, thoughtful, and patient; she is charming company. At fifteen, I was none of these. I was too unhappy to even contemplate feeling grateful—and I was certainly not charming, or kind. I had no use for anyone or anything but a few friends, and a boyfriend I was desperate to please. My life with my boyfriend was like falling down a well: I was in freefall all that year and the next. He treated me badly; I allowed myself to be treated badly.

Even my grandmother, whom I loved so, was cast out during this period. I had other things—too many things, I thought—on my mind. I couldn't be bothered with her. This didn't last long in the greater scheme of things, but it must have been very hard on her, perhaps harder on her than on anyone else (though it was no picnic for my parents): she and I had been the members of a mutual adoration society for fifteen years, and abruptly I'd resigned from the club. Still, I can't remember her complaining, not even afterward—although once, I recall, when I was nineteen or twenty, she gave me a beautiful sweater she had made in the 1940s, and I wondered aloud at its poor condition, for it looked abused, with a scattering of tiny stains, buttons missing or loose, one cuff unraveling. Everything else she had saved and handed on to me (one piece at a time, always making an occasion of it) was pristine, if yellowed—that is, you could always tell it was something old, but it had been perfectly preserved, wrapped in tissue and plastic shopping bags, a bundle secured with rubber bands. When I asked about the sweater, she gave me a hard look. "Once before, I gave this sweater to you. You don't remember? You wore it for some months or a year, and then one day you left it. You were so careless, you didn't even know you had left it. So I put it away again. But by then"—and she shrugged; she didn't have to finish, to say, "it was already ruined." She let the sentence dangle. She didn't have to point out, either, that the year in question was the year I was fifteen.

When *she* was fifteen, she left her home in Poland, in a small *shtetl* called Wysokie Mazowieckie, and traveled by herself to the U.S. It was 1913. Two years later she'd be married; two years after that, she'd have the first of her four children.

Grace was just over six months old when my grandmother died. They met only that one time, when I flew back to New York with her when she was three months old. I took pictures of that meeting, but something was wrong with the camera—it was a new camera, a small one I thought would be easier to manage when traveling with the baby than my bulky old 35 mm SLR. None of the pictures came out: the film was blank. So there is no record of their meeting, and no one but me to remember it. I tell the story of that day to Grace again and again, and while she doesn't pretend that this is news to her, she never says, "You've told me this before," as I surely would have at her age. She just listens.

I talk about my grandmother all the time, and not just to Grace. I talk about both my grandparents—to Grace, to my husband, to my mother and my brother, to friends who knew them and friends who didn't. I dream about both of them, too, though when my grandfather shows up in my dreams, my grandmother is always present as well, at least by implication or reference (offstage, as it were). When I dream of my grandmother, my grandfather is often gone—as he was in real life, of course, for the last decade of my grandmother's life. But long before his death, I saw her without him far more often than I saw him without her. Even in his old age, many years after he'd retired from what he always referred to as "the hat business"—a job in a garment center factory—he kept himself busy and was always "running out of the house," as my grandmother said disapprovingly.

I was twenty-seven when he died, of a massive stroke. It happened while he was out, walking on Brighton Beach Avenue. For years, my grandmother had been fearful every time he left "the house," their tiny one-bedroom apartment on Brighton Fifth. She waited and worried while he did the grocery shopping or went to the post office or the bank or took a walk on the boardwalk (which she considered an especially unnecessary risk, since this was an errand he sent himself on, for nothing but his own pleasure). When the news came to her on the day he collapsed, she said, "I knew it. I always knew it."

Not long ago I had a dream in which he had gone out to do the grocery shopping, as usual, but in the dream, he was young(er), more vigorous than he had been for many years, and I was with him, which I cannot remember ever happening in life (when I visited my grand-parents, I waited at home with my grandmother while he shopped, and he would bring home treats and produce them from his shop-ping cart with great fanfare: chocolate-covered graham crackers, ginger ale—which he always mixed with plain seltzer, carefully, be-fore drinking—Mallomars, Marshmallow Twists, ice cream). In the dream, however, my grandmother was dead—in this dream, it was she who had died first, and this had happened so long ago, the grief was no longer fresh—and he and I were arm in arm, chatting com-panionably as we turned the corner, walking from the boardwalk to Brighton Fifth Street, approaching the building where they had lived for decades, my "homeplace." But in the dream he didn't live there anymore, although in life I had never known him to live anywhere else. In the dream he remarked, as we passed the old building, that my grandmother was inside, alone and sick. I was astounded. How could he have kept this secret? How could I not have known? "I want to see her," I told him. "I need to go up and see her *right now*."

"No, no, you can't," he said. "It's too late at night. She'll be getting ready for bed. You'll frighten her."

"But I haven't seen her for so long," I said. I was crying. "Please. I *need* to see her. I would have gone before if only I'd known."

He held my arm tighter. "You didn't know. It's all right. You'll go another time. This is not the right time."

Even in the dream I was sure I'd never have the chance—that I'd missed my chance, that it was already too late.

When I woke up and remembered that they were both dead—when I understood that I'd been dreaming—I was confused. The grief I'd felt at the end of the dream was mixed up with the pleasure of having seen my grandfather again. I'd seen him, walked with him, touched him, listened to him! And the sweetness of running his errands with him, for once! And, oh, he was so healthy and happy, and the dream had felt—as dreams do—so *real*.

That I hadn't known *he* was alive until I was walking with him in the old neighborhood didn't even occur to me until later in the day. That surprise hadn't been part of the dream, so it wasn't part of what I was feeling when I woke from it. It was a delayed surprise. That I had twice been informed that what I thought was gone, wasn't gone—once while asleep, once while awake—left me feeling strangely reassured instead of disquieted. *So it's all right after all,* was what I caught myself thinking. *It's all right despite everything.*

Surprise weaves in and out of my dreams about my grandparents. Sometimes I am amazed to see them. "I didn't know you were still alive!" I say, and I weep over the missed years—years and years when I could have been spending time with them, if only I had known. In one dream, my grandfather, who appeared to be in his seventies, the age he was when I was a teenager—although in the dream I was the age I am now—patted my arm and said, "Don't worry about it, *mamaleh.* I've been fine, it's all right. And I'm here now, so let's just enjoy the time we have together" (exactly the sort of thing he would have said in real life). But more often, I haven't even *mistakenly* thought they were dead: real life is entirely absent. I'm not surprised to see them, because in the dream they hadn't died (as in the dream of running errands with my grandfather), and never mind that the year is now and I am my own age—which would mean that my grandfather would, in real-world time, have lived nearly to the Jewish proverbial age of 120: *May you live to 120,* we say—*may you live as long as Moses did.* (This, I feel obliged to note, is the kind of dream [il]logic that leads Hobson to pronounce dreaming to be psychosis.)

I am always so glad to see my grandfather in my dreams—just as I was always glad to see him in real life. An uncomplicated gladness: I cannot remember ever being irritated or impatient with him, or arguing with him—or even disagreeing with him (by which I don't mean merely contradicting him; I mean that even in the privacy of my own mind, I had no cause to disagree). I was crazy about him; I loved him uncritically, with all my heart. I was charmed by, delighted by, everything about him. But it's also true that I didn't *know* him as I knew my grandmother. He didn't tell me his secrets (he seemed not to have any—which surely cannot have been true). I never told him mine, either. My grandmother had been an extra mother to me when I was a small child (and sometimes altogether a substitute mother) and later on more friend than mother or grandmother, even as I played the role of extra grown daughter to both her and my grandfather—taking them to their appointments with doctors, checking in by phone whether I felt like it or not. My grandfather and I certainly never talked for hours, and never on the phone. He and I would sit at the kitchen table and he would take my hands in his and say, "Tell me, are you happy?" Or: "Tell me, are you managing to make a good living?" He never complained about my grandmother—not once. *My love,* he called her when he spoke of her to me. *My beauty, my sweetheart. Mayn basherter*—my predestined one. He admired her; he *adored* her.

He was my admirer, too, and he was always gentle, even courtly, with me. When I was eighteen, and he was in his eighties, during a summer I spent working at the deli counter of a Waldbaum's supermarket, he would sometimes take the subway from Brighton Beach to Avenue M—five stops—just for the pleasure of seeing me out in the world. He would come into the store and stand silently watching me work, as if I were putting on a show (slicing cold cuts by machine, carving lox with a long, sharp knife).

Neither of my parents—nor my grandmother for that matter—would ever have done such a thing. None of them would ever even have thought of doing such a thing.

For a moment, when I wake up after I have dreamt that my grandfather is alive, in those first few seconds before my ordinary waking life resumes, I believe that it was his death that was "just a dream." How foolish of me to think he was gone! And then suddenly I am awake enough to know better. I'm not really shocked, or even disappointed. It happens in a flash, and I have been accustomed to his death for so long it isn't difficult to become readjusted to it. On the contrary—all day, on those days, I feel happier than usual. There's a part of me that still feels what I felt in the dream and when I first woke from it. And I believe that this is at least partly why I dream of my grandparents so often: to remind myself that I still have what I am so often sure I don't have anymore.

I believe it was that reassurance that stayed with me after I got out of bed *this* morning, after my dream about my grandmother. That it wasn't a "good" dream (that even the "good parts"—the discovery that my grandmother was still alive, or how lovely, how *gorgeous,* she became when she was surrounded by people she loved—were shaded dark, so that inside the shell of every bit of good news was a core of bleak, alarming news) didn't matter so much as the *still here after all* did.

It turns out that dreaming that someone or something has returned, or is still around after all, is not uncommon. Nor is dreaming that you have something you never knew you had in the first place—which often takes the form of an "extra rooms" scenario, in which you wander down a hall or open a door you'd never noticed before at home (in the real world), and you find that there's a room, or several rooms, you never knew existed. This is a "good" dream, a dream most people enjoy having (even if it makes them a little uneasy: *how could I not have known about this?*). It isn't hard to interpret, either, in its basic outline: *Look at what I have! Look at these possibilities I didn't even know existed!*

I have this dream—some variation of this dream—more often than seems reasonable (how many hidden possibilities can there *be*? After a certain number of years, you'd think you would have uncovered all of them—just as you'd think you'd know about the extra rooms by now if you've been living in the same house, as I now have, for nearly twenty years).

When I have this dream, it's nearly always a basement that leads to what amounts to a whole *houseful* of rooms I didn't know I had—room after room, furnished and abandoned. There is evidence everywhere of the rooms having been lived in—and not just lived in, but well used: books scattered, dishes left on tables, towels carelessly rehung in the bathroom, pillows stacked on couches, the couch cushions softly indented. I walk from room to room—stunned, thrilled, discomfited, aware that I have to readjust the way I think about my house, now that I have a whole extra house's worth of rooms. *What am I to do with them?* I think, and, *Oh, there are so many things I might do with them!*

I wake up amazed, excited, puzzled, anxious. I know this is good news. I'm not the least ambivalent about the extra space—I know I can make good use of it (even *in* the dream I think, *This is just what I've been needing!*)—but it feels like a burden, too (there's work to be done; there are decisions to be made). And rumbling beneath both the pleasure and the dread, there is a question, an accusation: *What's wrong with me? I should have known all this was here. I should have been attending to it.* And finally there's a layer—a thin layer but it's there, nonetheless, beneath the layers of anxiety and perplexity and pleasure—of dismay, regret: *What good use I would have made of all this if only I had known before!*

A "good" dream, then, with a gloomy underside.

For over thirty years I've also had a variation of this type of dream that seems to bring no good news at all, one that gives the surprise-room scenario a grim twist. In this dream, there is a door that leads, most often, to a rooftop—a city roof, an apartment building roof, flat, tarred, with built-up edges, a roof you'd have to work at falling off (first you'd have to climb, in order to fall)—but sometimes the door is in a basement, a cellar, like the one in my "extra rooms" dreams, except that it leads to just one room and it's one I *knew* was there. It's what's in it that's a surprise. Whether on the roof or in the cellar, what I find are cages filled with animals—terrible cages, in poor repair. Like the cages in the old zoos in New York City, in the days before zoo animals were confined in "environments." The cages have paint-chipped, rusting metal bars. (I realize only now, as I am writing about them, that the cages remind me of the apartment, the building complex itself, where my grandmother spent her last years, alone—that I have even invoked the same word, "terrible," to describe them.)

There are cages everywhere I turn, and in every cage there is an animal, and it is starving, near dead (yes, like my grandmother in last night's dream before the presence of her family brought her back to life, however temporarily). These are animals I didn't know I had, or else once knew I had but had forgotten. There are all kinds of animals—it depends on the night, on the particular dream. Sometimes they are wild animals, sometimes domestic or farm animals. There are small animals and large—sometimes gigantic—animals. There are zoo animals, circus animals that have been retired, pets (dogs, cats, birds, reptiles) I seemed to have acquired without being aware of it—and thus hadn't known I was supposed to care for—and pets I'd surely once known I had but had somehow lost track of.

I wake from these dreams regretful, frightened, despairing. I wake up groaning, thinking *not again.* The tigers have been starved down to skin and bones and patches of striped fur *again.* Missing teeth, sunken eyes.

Tigers, owls, lions, peacocks, panting dogs—all of them skeletal, exhausted, lying on their sides in their filthy cages. Again.

But sometimes there are no cages. There are still animals all around me—animals I'd neglected, abandoned, but that remain with me, under my care—and they are roaming free. Prowling. Starving. The cats I had for many years in real life, both of them long dead now, come back to me in my dreams (all these years I hadn't fed them—*I didn't know! Where have they been?*).

Or I dream of discovering that my cats are still alive but that although I haven't fed them they are surprisingly *not* starving. What have they been eating? How have they managed to stay alive all this time? In the dream I promise myself to begin feeding them regularly, now that I know they are still with me—but *still* I forget. Days and weeks pass in the dream and I cannot seem to remember to keep cat food in the house, or to fill their dishes and set them down if I do have food, any kind of food, for them.

And yet they do not die. They aren't well, I can see that. They're not *robust*, I think in the dream. But although they're moving slowly—they're too thin, they're fragile—they're *still here* (like my grandmother in what I am already thinking of as the *starving-grandmother* dream). They must be scavenging, I think. Or else they don't *need* food. Perhaps that's it—and in the dream this is a revelation: the need for food is an illusion, or a lie; it's something we've been told is true which isn't. The cats can live on air; they can live on nothing.

In real life, Cadence, the older of my two cats, whom I adopted when she was already in cat midlife, in 1977, died the same week a man I loved broke up with me, in 1989—abruptly, devastatingly, without any warning. Cadence was ancient by then, and she had no teeth; I bought her jars of Earth's Best baby food and woke her up to coax her to eat. Elizabeth—Lizzy—who was a kitten when I brought her home in the winter of 1976, died four years after Cadence did. For months she'd been so frail she'd had to be carried around the house, lifted into the litter box, lifted onto the couch to sleep beside me while I nursed my newborn baby daughter. I fed Lizzy baby food, too—with her various medications mixed into it—but *svet gornisht helfen*, as my grandmother would have said, and she was gone by the time Grace was four months old. My grandmother died two months later.

But in my dreams, my grandmother is back, my cats are back—the boyfriend who broke up with me in 1989 is back, as is my high school boyfriend, as is my first apartment, as are streets I haven't walked on in four decades. Everything gets to come back in dreams — the people and places you're glad to see again and the ones you'd hoped you never would. Everything is still there, still alive, in our dreams. Whether we want it to be or not.

3

Even when my cats were still alive, I dreamed of them. Mostly I had "bad" dreams about them (they were lost, or they were sick, or they had died—and more than once I dreamed that *I* had accidentally killed one of them, spraying her with roach poison I'd misaimed)—but then most dreams are bad dreams, according to Hobson (whose research suggests that two-thirds of our dreams are "negative") and other scientists (the research team of Calvin Hall and Robert Van de Castle reported a figure of eighty percent, of more than five hundred "dream reports" they collected in 1966 for their book, *The Content Analysis of Dreams*).

It makes sense to me that most of our dreams would be bad (full of "negative emotions," as Hall and Van de Castle put it), though not necessarily for the reasons offered by the sleep scientists. They believe that having bad dreams is good for evolutionary fitness: if our dreams serve the purpose of allowing us to rehearse threatening scenarios, then those of us who have more (and more vivid) bad dreams would be better prepared for trouble when it comes—and thus would be more likely to survive those real-life threats to become "the progenitors of offspring," as the psychologists Michael Franklin and Michael Zyphur explain in a 2005 article, "The Role of Dreams in the Evolution of the Human Mind," in the journal *Evolutionary Psychology*. Franklin and Zyphur drew on the work of Hall and Van de Castle as well as Hobson and others to conclude that the ability to have vividly bad dreams, plus a propensity toward such dreams, is probably "differentially passed on to future generations."

And perhaps it is. But it also seems plain to me that the things that are troubling us—or the *kinds* of things that are troubling us—tend to preoccupy us. We may be able to suppress that preoccupation when we're awake, by dint of sheer effort (though I suppose the most congenitally upbeat of us can keep our minds on the good news without trying, and the most congenitally downbeat can't do it no matter how hard they try), but once we're asleep, all bets are off: the bad news comes pouring in for all of us.

There's no reason to assume that the evolutionary fitness explanation and this one are mutually exclusive. There may well be an adaptive advantage to being inclined toward worry and stress; it may be that bad news always makes the front page because that's what's important in the evolutionary scheme of things (so that even if we hold the paper open to the sports pages or the comics, in repose the paper flutters closed again, and there are those grim headlines, however scrambled). But then the function of our dreams would only be an extension of our overall bad news-processing apparatus—which I believe is more likely to be true than not, and which is just another way of saying that I'd rather not hold dreams separate from everything else about ourselves, which, it strikes me, is what the sleep scientists insist on doing (for what other activity do we engage in regularly that a scientist would discount as "trash"?).

In any case, it doesn't seem strange to me that my dreams about my cats when they were still alive were usually bad ones, or that so many of the bad dreams I had, when my cats were still with me, featured them. The cats were excellent stand-ins for aspects of myself (or to make concrete in some other way whatever it was I was struggling with) because I was so deeply attached to them, as people who live alone with their pets for a long time often are. (Of course, I have been married and a mother for many years now, and I am *still* deeply attached—pathologically attached, my husband will sometimes say—to the pets we live with, Molly the dog and Cody the bird. And I dream about them, too, just as I used to—and continue to, so many years after their deaths—dream about Cadence and Lizzy.)

My sleeping mind, in fact, is a veritable bestiary. Aside from the pets, contemporary and past, the caged animals, the starving animals, I have dreamed about ducks, about cats *other* than my own, about domesticated birds other than Cody, about infestations—both of the ordinary kind (mice) and extraordinary kinds (chickens, frogs)—and, strangely often, about big brown bears. (I once dreamed I was in a race with one. And once a big brown bear visited me, sitting down on my dining room table rather delicately but taking up all the room, making a sort of nest for itself there.)

Animals, other than my own pets, do not play an especially important role in my life. Except for one horrifying true-life mouse invasion a few years ago, which taught me a lesson about tidiness I have followed religiously since, and the roaches I had to contend with three decades ago in my first apartment, I haven't spent any waking time thinking about or experiencing infestation. My experience of frogs is limited to the large collection of plastic ones my daughter played with when she was very young, and the yearly retrieval of them from the bin of assorted toy animals in the basement for our Passover seder, when everyone at the table is issued a handful to throw when the second plague, *tzefardeyah* (after *dam*, the water turning into blood, but before *kinim*, the Egyptians afflicted with lice), is mentioned.

Why, then, do animals turn up so often in my dream life?

I should confess, before I try to answer this question, that sometimes I find myself thinking of my dreams as if they really *were* written—or directed, or painted, or composed—by someone else; as if, to fully appreciate them, I need to look at them not only individually but also as a whole (what are the recurring themes? which metaphors turn up again and again? what is it, really, that this author—this artist—is preoccupied with?). I should confess, too, that the provenance of dream imagery is as interesting to me as are dream narratives themselves. It surprises me how incurious most people (even enthusiastic dream-interpreters) seem to be about the origin of dream metaphors. Leaving aside—for the moment, anyway—those who dismiss entirely the significance of the symbols in our dreams (that they are symbols at all, rather than randomly generated images, and that examining them for clues about what we're feeling or experiencing that we're largely unaware of during our waking life—*real life*, as we say—is a worthwhile enterprise), I wonder about the separation of plot from other elements of dreams (as if dreams were more like science fiction or romance or horror novels than like *Middlemarch* or *Anna Karenina*). Of course, many of the unconscious "choices" made in our dreams seem to be archetypal, or very nearly so (I'm thinking now of dream imagery of rooms, houses, physical paralysis, teeth, flight, falling), so it's easy to see how they might not be thought of as especially revealing of one's own unique unconscious "character" or of pervasive themes. Still, one can parse even these archetypal symbols. Virtually all of us have strong feelings about the place where we live, and about *having* a place to live: why wouldn't we make use of this in some way as we re-imagine ourselves and our lives while we sleep? That so many people dream about being unable to move isn't much of a mystery, either (no more than it's a mystery to me that I *don't* make use of this metaphor in my dreams, since physical activity, other than at its most basic level, has never been of much importance or interest to me). For anyone who has ever participated in a sport, or who has or has ever had a physically taxing job, or whose idea of recreation is hiking or ballroom dancing, what would be a more useful symbol of feeling trapped or helpless? When *I* am in despair, on the other hand, I am more likely to dream about telephones that don't work—to dream of racing from pay phone to pay phone (a metaphor of my own generation: even though I've used a cell phone for years now, cell phones never turn up in my dreams, as if it is too late for my mind to accommodate a new symbol, especially when I have a perfectly suitable one already filed away) and finding all of them broken (and if one happens to work, I instantly forget the number I had meant to call). It's being unable to have a conversation that horrifies *me*, that serves to represent a version of the-worst-thing-that-can-happen.

How are we to make sense of our own metaphor-making machinery? For my own purposes, I rely on association and instinct. My pets are easy metaphors for me: they do, in real life, feel like extensions of myself. I identify and empathize with them; I *count* on them—and, in exchange for their dependability, I over-indulge them. (I might take this a step further and consider *why* this is so—why I am so devoted to and involved with my pets—and make the further effort to pair this consideration with my stronger-than-many's need for communication, or communion—but this is perhaps not the time or place for that piece of self-analysis.) Animals other than my pets (all those lions and tigers and bears!) are more puzzling to me. I am not an especially fervent animal rights advocate, or even a vegetarian. Nor am I a hunter. Or a nature photographer, stalking animals with a camera. I don't hang calendars that feature adorable animals, or awe-inspiring animals-in-the-wild scenes taken by other people's cameras. I don't care for zoos.

How am I to understand the frequent appearance of animals in my dream life, then?

Here is the only way I know to try to:

I close my eyes and do my best to stop thinking in an organized, focused way. I set aside my knowledge—my reflexive certainty—that such animals as appear in my dreams are not of (conscious) significance to me. I allow my mind to wander freely around the *idea* of animals and pay attention to the feelings that begin to rise to the surface as I do. This is less "free association" (as Freud called it) than "free-feeling," although it's quite true that spontaneous thoughts arise as well as emotions. I don't make an effort to suppress thoughts when they come—out of the quiet, as it were—but I don't chase them, either. I am not after anything definitive; I am not even after *insight*. I am trying to understand the recurring images in my dreams the way I might understand my experience of a galleryful of a painter's work. Not "why do I like—or do not like—this?" Not even "why does it make me feel what I am feeling?" But simply "*how* does it make me feel?"

When I quiet my effortful, thinking self around the "idea" of animals, what comes out of the quiet is this:

Admiration. Appreciation. Respect. Wonder.
Strength. Power.
Unknowability.
Danger.

Danger? "Danger" is a surprise. In my dreams the animals are never dangerous. There is sometimes the *implication* of danger, but there is never an actual threat. Even the big brown bears of my dreams are not threatening. They are only mysterious, and *difficult*. Indeed, all the animals are mysterious and difficult in one way or another. My own pets—so well-known in life—when they appear in my dreams, turn mysterious. I am impressed with them, but I don't understand them; I don't believe I *can* understand them.

Now, I am willing to take for granted that the various animals are stand-ins for parts, or aspects, of myself; I take for granted that anything we dream about, any metaphors our dream-making machinery concocts, represents ourselves, less whole than in part. But what parts of myself are showing up (repeatedly, for decades) in these dreams?

Neglected or abandoned parts, it seems certain. But also the most interesting, admirable, difficult, mysterious, and potentially dangerous parts. The parts of myself I don't even know about.

And that creatures about which I don't have particularly strong conscious feelings or thoughts should so often be entrusted by my unconscious to fulfill such an important role seems to me to do double metaphorical duty—metaphor once removed: the caged, starving animals I can't imagine how I didn't know I had (I don't ever ask myself, in my dreams, *how* they came to be mine—who put them in those cages on that rooftop?—only how it is that I could not have known they were!), the huge bears, so famously dangerous (but not to me, not in this context), that insist on being contended with, are not even the *symbols* I would have chosen if my waking mind were in charge.

I am interested, too, in the dream-symbols at the other end of the spectrum: the ones that are so obvious I am ashamed to have reached for them, even in my sleep (or *especially* in my sleep—because although I joke that the clichés that so often turn up in my dreams reassure me that I'm in close touch with my unconscious—*see? my mind's an open book to me*—I fear that they may suggest a sort of pure simplemindedness that is otherwise hidden away even from me).

Falling flat on my face, being in over my head, just missing the boat—these are the kinds of dreams that embarrass me, even when I don't talk to anyone about them (I am *privately* embarrassed; don't let anybody try to tell you this isn't possible). In a novella I wrote as I was nearing fifty, I gave some of my most literal-minded (or simpleminded) dreams to my protagonist (how relieved I was to give them away!). She was a character for whom—or on whom—these dreams would be a good joke: a poet—someone whose life's work was the making of complex, elegant metaphors. (And just to make the joke complete—privately complete—my poet was a woman whose relationship with a pet is a stand-in for all other possible relationships.)

I've heard of people who dream of skeletons in their closets, of making their beds and then lying in them, of flying under the radar. The best literal-minded dream *I* have ever had was about wrestling with a bear—one of my big brown bears, naturally. I dreamed of the bear as the publication date for my first nonfiction book was approaching, and I told a friend about it—told him because I thought the metaphor my sleeping mind had come up with was genuinely funny. I said, "You know that phrase, 'it's a bear,' don't you, for something that's uncommonly difficult?" He did. "It's not even a phrase I would ever *use*," I told him. "It sounds to me like something slangy a college student might say. But not one of my own students, because it sounds so old-fashioned. It must be a bit of *old* slang — from when *we* were young, maybe?" "Maybe," he said. I knew this wasn't the sort of question that interested him (except for other writers — and my daughter — no one I know is interested in this sort of question), so I hurried on to talk about how worried I only just then (thanks to my dream!) understood I was about the book. I had high hopes for it, I said, which I had been trying to keep in check — *don't expect anything, don't expect anything*: that's my mantra when it comes to publishing — but at the same time I was terrifically anxious about publishing it at all (something else I'd been trying not to think about), since I told secrets about myself and my family in it. "And really — good lord — just resolving *those* two things seems impossible! Thinking this could be *the* book, and feeling as if it shouldn't even *be* a book. It's no wonder I was rolling around on the floor with a big brown bear." And my friend — an efficient, practical-minded, no-nonsense sort of person, a scientist who spends his days running a lab and writing grants to keep it running — said, "You know, sometimes I think you have too much time on your hands." I was stunned. While it's easy to keep in mind that certain of my passions and preoccupations are not universally shared, I often forget that not everyone (not even everyone I know and like) looks at things the way I do — that not everyone finds this sort of analysis and reflection the best use of one's time. I don't understand why everyone does not. I was shocked, not long ago, to learn that "rumination" is widely considered to be a *bad* thing.

After the book came out (a trying, exhilarating, painful, thrilling, *interesting* time, because not only was everything about that book — writing it, finding a publisher for it, waiting for it to come out, dealing with my complicated feelings about it once it did — *a bear*, but I published a novella, the one about the literal-minded dreamer/poet, that same month, and the publisher of *that* book decided to market it as a novel, which I feared would set up the wrong expectations about it, *and* I turned fifty, which somehow came as a shock to me, and I coped with my shock by throwing myself a big party, which my younger brother helped to pay for, and then he nearly died, the night of the party, and kept on nearly dying for days afterward, and then at last recovered, miraculously), I had one of my animals-in-cages dreams. It was different from any of the others, though—as befits a time in my life that was different from any other—because this time all the animals were well cared for. None of them were starving; I'd known all along that I was responsible for them.

There was one particularly vivid image in the dream. One of the caged animals was a tiger—a very small but powerful tiger. And in the dream I was aware that it was unwise to be keeping a tiger, even fenced in this way (that was the word I used in the dream: *fenced*—not caged). There was a problem with the fence, too. Every time I looked, it was a little more torn down. The tiger was too small to be dangerous, I was sure, but still it was impossible to know what kind of damage it might do if it escaped. And then suddenly the tiger had vanished; in its place was something harmless—a puppy? (when I woke, I wasn't sure; I was sure only that it was something nice, something that *couldn't* do any harm, that was just barely old enough to be without its mother). At once it was clear to me that the person responsible for the removal of the tiger was my daughter's beloved social studies teacher (the only good teacher Grace had that year—in all of middle school, in fact: an oasis of kindness and intellectual rigor in a desert of meanness and small-minded, middlebrow dullness). Mrs. Rosenbaum, it emerged, had volunteered coolly to "shoot it dead." This was astonishing. Mrs. Rosenbaum is not only not the sort of person to shoot anything, but the phrase "shoot it dead" was so unlike her that even in the dream I was surprised. "It was too dangerous to keep it," she told me gently.

I woke up in a tangle of emotions, none of them news to me. Did I need a dream about a well-tended, ineffectively set-apart, potentially dangerous, powerful, beautiful, small thing from which I was unexpectedly rescued by my daughter's good teacher to tell me about my anxiety, fear, sadness, relief, gratitude, pride—and all the rest of what I was feeling—as I waited for reviews of my books to appear, as I did my best to make peace with being fifty, as my brother was brought back from the brink of death? As I waited to hear (I was so sure I would hear) that I was a very bad mother, because of what I admitted in print about raising my daughter? As I waited to see if perhaps these two books coming out simultaneously would finally (*oh, but they won't, they won't*) "make" my career? As I castigated myself for caring. As I wondered if it were too late to matter. As I contemplated the extraordinary fact that students from nearly two decades of my teaching career had gathered, along with my childhood friends, along with my mother and my daughter and all of *their* closest friends, in a ballroom, in gowns and black tie, to celebrate my birthday. Mrs. Rosenbaum, as it happened, had been there too. *That* was how much I liked her, how grateful I was to her for whatever she had been able to do for my daughter.

Had I not been (as the pop-psychology saying goes) "in touch with" those feelings?

I don't think so. I would say that I was *constantly* "in touch with" all of those feelings in my waking life. I knew exactly how I felt. I even had a pretty good idea of why I felt it. What the dream seemed to offer me was something else, something that went deeper than feelings. Something darker and more convoluted than even the convoluted brew of all those feelings mixed up together.

I found myself lingering on the image of the caged small tiger: it was a glorious creature, small as a cub but somehow full grown, and *fearsomely* strong, I could tell, pacing in its cage that wouldn't contain it much longer, clearly more dangerous than my dream-self had assumed it to be. My dream-self wasn't thinking about danger at all; it—she—was only worried about containing the tiger for its own sake, keeping *it* safe.

I pictured the puppy—the puppylike creature, whatever it was, smaller even than the tiger, smaller by far, and *obviously* harmless, a complete innocent, newly weaned from its mother—that had taken the tiger's place.

Thinking about the dream this way was more Jungian than Freudian—for Jung was adamant about the personal relevance of symbols (which he referred to as *signs*, distinguishing them from archetypes, which he not only acknowledged but celebrated). He insisted that his patients, as they recalled their dreams, focus on the images themselves, rather than "free associating" *from* the images (the simplest way to differentiate their approaches—perhaps an unfairly simple way, a demarcation in a nutshell—is to say that Freud believed that dreams had the potential to reveal the truth behind the lies of our conscious thought processes, in particular our secret wishes, which nearly always led to revelations of repressed sexuality, and Jung thought of dreams as having their own purpose, their own logic, as interesting on their own terms as our conscious purposes and logic). Jung would ask his patients to re-imagine their dreams and describe each image to him as if they had never seen such a thing before.

That was what I tried to do, describing the images to myself, as I went back over my dream. Instead of thinking about what the caged (or *fenced-in*, as the dream defined it) tiger suggested to me, instead of associating freely about tigers—or puppies, or good teachers—I allowed myself to be still and to re-imagine, for a moment, the small tiger in its disintegrating pen. It startled me to see it, then: to see what I hadn't considered in the dream—that its size was so deceptive; that its size had no relation to its strength. It only *looked* small; it wasn't small at all—its apparent size was irrelevant. Its power was in fact terrifying—and only a fence (not even a proper cage—not even one of my "usual" cages) was keeping it from doing great harm, even as I believed that the fence was keeping it safe *for me* (it was my tiger; I didn't want it to go anywhere, to get away).

And that fence was being torn down incrementally (without my knowing it; every time I looked, there was less fence to see), which would have been a disaster if the danger it had been containing had not been eliminated by the brave and surprising act of "the good teacher" (and what, I had to ask myself—automatically taking up Freud's method now—did I think about when I thought about that phrase, that idea: "the good teacher"? Why, I hardly needed to *free* associate at all: I had been thinking a great deal lately about how being a teacher, and being good at being a teacher, had—unexpectedly—come to be as central to my understanding of who I was as being a writer had been for nearly all of my life. Hadn't I just been feted by former students who had traveled from farflung places in order to be with me? The truth was that even when I felt I was failing as a writer or a mother—and just then I was full of fear that I was failing at the former and had written a book about the ways I'd failed at the latter—I remained confident in myself, in my *goodness*, as a teacher). Why, I had come to my own rescue, I thought, hadn't I? I'd written that book and turned something dangerous into something I could live with. (I even laughed, when I arrived at this, for in the dream the "something I could live with" seemed to be a puppy: precisely the creature the character in my *other* book had adopted, and which had, in its way, saved *her* life.)

I thought also about the word *middle* (as in middle school teacher; as in middle age; as in *The Middle of Everything*—the title of the nonfiction book that had just come out, the book I was so anxious about) and about separation from a mother (the puppy in the dream; my book's account of both Grace's delayed separation from me, and my own enforced separation from my depressed mother). I thought about how my usual methods for keeping things under control weren't working (the falling-apart cage that wasn't even a cage to begin with). I thought about how in this dream, as opposed to every other dream I could remember ever having about caged animals, I wasn't neglecting anything: I knew what I had, and I'd been taking care of it (even if I didn't really understand it—even if I were denying its true nature).

I thought about cages and fences and crates for puppies and cribs for babies, about puppies, about tigers the size of cubs, and about my own little brother—my "little" brother who is a powerful man, a broadcasting executive, formally recognized as one of the "Ten Most Powerful People in Radio"—whose generosity and kindness to me, in our adulthood, is both legion and undeserved. In our childhood, I treated him badly. When he was left in my charge, I neglected him (and once, the story goes, I tried to kill him—but I was only four; I'm not sure that threatening him in his crib with my sneaker counts as the attempted murder of the family anecdote), but for the most part, I simply ignored him, behaving as if he didn't exist. And now, suddenly, as I'd turned fifty, when he was forty-six, he had almost ceased to.

In short, the imagery and narrative of my dream, as I allowed myself to re-imagine each image and also free-associate from the images and narrative (that is, a little bit of Jung, a little bit of Freud), let me in on some things to which I wouldn't have had conscious access without having had (and interpreted) the dream. I didn't need the dream to let me know what I was feeling—but until I had the dream I didn't know very much about where those feelings had come from; I didn't know what they meant.

In their own ways, Freud and Jung—who began as mentor and apprentice, metaphorically father and son, and ended in enmity (Jung accusing Freud of dogmatism and, by implication, grandiosity; Freud dismissing Jung's "mysticism" and accusing him, the wayward son, of wishing him, the father, dead) — both tell us that if we listen hard enough, our dreams can whisper to us of all manner of things we would not otherwise know.

Hobson would snort with derision at such a statement. He has devoted much of his career to rescuing dreams from the notion that they should be examined for their content, for meaning, particularly for hints about what he mockingly calls "hidden feelings." There is no mystery to dreams, he declares. In place of "dream mystique," he has written, "we aim to install dream science."

Perhaps I reject what Hobson says about dreams simply because it is so *uninteresting*.

4

ere is a paradox, speaking of what is interesting and what is not: that our dreams are so interesting to us—those who dream them (even to the professional Freud-debunkers among us)—and yet nobody wants to hear them. And we *know* this; and still we can't resist telling them.

(What a comedy! Nobody wants to hear anybody else's dreams; everybody wants to tell his dreams to somebody.)

But I'm exaggerating. *Somebody* wants—or had once wanted—to hear your dreams. Your mother, when you were a child. Your best friend, at fourteen. Anyone newly in love with you, at any age. If you're lucky, the person you're married to, year in, year out (but take care: tell too *many* dreams, too many mornings in a row, and he will join the ranks of the uninterested, especially if he never turns up *in* these dreams, or appears only as a villain).

At the very least, there are always psychoanalysts, who can be counted on to ask, "Any dreams?" and to listen (or appear to listen) when their patients recount them. Often they even take notes. What more could a dreamer ask?

My daughter and I, for many years, would start the day by telling each other our dreams. We'd roll our eyes over the too-obvious metaphors we were both prone to ("Like I needed a dream to tell me *that*," Grace, not quite fourteen, would say after reporting that she was on a narrow ledge and knew she was supposed to jump—or that she'd been handed the keys to a car and she was frightened, then suddenly realized she *did* know how to drive after all).

Until very recently, Grace was, like me, the kind of person who remembered her dreams nearly every morning—remembered multiple dreams, and in considerable detail—but in the full bloom of her adolescence, her dreams have begun to go underground. This may be due at least in part to her not getting enough sleep (here I will nod to the sleep scientists), but also, I think, it's because of the turmoil of adolescence itself: it is as if she has quite enough to deal with while *awake.* These days sleeping itself is an afterthought, a luxury, four or five hours whipped off after a late night of studying.

She will sometimes talk wistfully about the days when she woke up with a head full of dreams. Not that she always enjoyed dreaming. When she was five, she told me once that she *hated* dreaming. I was taken aback. "But dreams are a marvel," I said, "aren't they? All those stories playing inside your head?"

"But that's *exactly* what I hate," she said. "I hate that there's a movie inside your mind that plays and you have no control over it."

It has occurred to me that this anxiety about control may have some part too in her recent dream desert. If you don't remember your dreams, you don't have to contend with them—or with the "loss of control" that lets them come about in the first place. (And if there's anything a teenager has less of than a sense of control, I don't know what that would be. Although perhaps a teenager without the abiding need *for* control that Grace has had since early childhood would be less troubled by this.) It also strikes me now that when she suddenly decided that she "hated" dreams, she was about to start kindergarten—a transition even greater than the one she made at fourteen, when she started high school. And here's something else: the *last* major transition she made, from elementary to middle school, was marked by a once-in-a-lifetime dreaming event: she and I had matching dreams the night before school started.

That day, the day before her first day of sixth grade, of middle school, she and I had gone shopping for back-to-school clothes (boring, because her school had a dress code: we filled a cart with khaki pants and white and navy blue shirts) and shoes. But we'd also gotten (or *I'd* gotten—I was, after all, the one with the credit card) a little carried away over shoes. There were the shoes she needed—plain black comfortable shoes with a sensible heel—and there were the shoes we both decided she couldn't live without: hot pink sandals we found on the clearance rack; knee-high zip-up boots, the kind she'd "always wanted," she said earnestly; checkerboard-patterned slip-on sneakers . . . and then there was my own inability to wander through a store's shoe department without buying at least one pair. We left with a bagful of the dullest imaginable clothes, and five new pairs of shoes between us.

Straight from shopping, we met Grace's best friend, Kristin, and her mother, Carolyn, for a celebratory lunch. We went to an Indian restaurant—Grace's choice—and Kristin, who is a notoriously unadventurous eater, was willing for once to try all sorts of new things; Carolyn, who had been a little doubtful about the food herself, ended up enjoying it, too. Grace was happy because she'd made a choice everyone approved of, and she was happy because her friend was happy—Kristin's moods have always affected hers disproportionately—and she was happy because she had finished elementary school, which she'd hated, and she was full of hope (which would soon enough be dashed) about middle school. She was beaming as she doused everything on her plate with *raita*. "Everything is so *good*," she said. And it was.

Carolyn stopped eating after one trip to the buffet, commenting that she *could* eat more but she didn't "have to." I considered this (I was on plate number three). "*That's* why you're thin," I said (not much of a revelation, but it seemed like one at the time), "and I have to struggle so with my weight. I can always eat more and I always do, until I *can't*."

Carolyn laughed politely. But I was still thinking about this hours later—about how I'd always thought of my extravagance and expansiveness as among my "good" traits, but how, in middle age—at least when it came to food—it might be nice to be able to take a leaf out of *her* book. I was thinking, too, about how we'd gotten through the whole lunch without my mentioning the five pairs of shoes—or, for that matter, the hair appointment I'd made for Grace, at her request, following lunch, where she would get her very long, thick, wavy (in fact, one might call it "out of control") auburn hair washed and then flat-ironed into glossy submission. Grace (like her mother) feels prettier and more confident when her hair is straight, and for the last few years, for special occasions, I have offered her the option—a treat, an indulgence. The truth was that I would have been willing to do *anything* that might help to soothe her anxiety about going to school the next day. While she wasn't changing schools in the move from elementary to middle school, but merely changing hallways (the day would now be divided into separate classes, the children marching back and forth from one room to another in a single hallway in the small building), I knew that right along with her conviction that sixth grade would be a vast improvement over fifth, she was also nervous—worried about the changes ahead, *and* worried that things would not be as different as she hoped.

Still, the excess—or what I imagined might be considered excess—embarrassed me in the presence of Carolyn, who is so abstemious. It must have embarrassed Grace, too, because she didn't say anything about the shoes or the hair salon, either. After lunch, we just said we had "more to do," and the two pairs of mothers and daughters went their separate ways.

That night, after our day out, I dreamed that we'd come home from the salon and after dinner Grace had taken her evening shower, as usual—as indeed she had in real life, carefully tucking her hair into not one but three shower caps (as long as flat-ironed hair stays perfectly dry, it stays perfectly straight)—but in the dream she washed her hair. And I was furious at her. "I went to the trouble to take you to the salon!" I cried. "And I spent fifteen dollars! Fifteen dollars! Do you think that money is nothing? I'll take it out of your allowance! For five weeks you won't get a cent from me! That'll teach you what fifteen dollars is!"

In real life I had never once talked to her this way. In real life I would hear other mothers talking to their children this way and I would cringe. Sometimes it even made me cry. (I would turn away, to cry in secret—shocked, but ashamed of myself, too. *This is none of your business*, I would tell myself, but it didn't help, it didn't keep me from feeling awful. *Think of how you're making that child feel!* I'd think, and just barely manage to keep from saying.)

In my dream I was one of those mothers. Grace stayed calm; she shrugged as I berated her. She offered three explanations (three contradictory ones, in a row). She said, "It was an accident. I forgot." And she said, "I had so much trouble getting my hair in separate sections"—those were the words in the dream—"I finally just gave up, I couldn't get it all in the shower cap. I was frustrated and it was time to stop messing with it." And then she said, defiantly, "I like to wash my hair when I take a shower, okay?"

"Which is it?" I screamed at her. "It can't be all three! They cancel each other out!"

In the morning, when I finished telling her my dream (just the dream, not my editorializing: I didn't say anything about the bad mothers, the ones who made me cringe, or how much I'd hated myself for being one of them; I didn't even mention that "fifteen dollars" was not an accurate figure), she said, "This is too weird. *I* dreamed that we came home from my hair appointment and I got into the shower and washed my hair and you yelled at me, screaming like a crazy person."

She was still in bed; her eyes weren't even all the way open. She'd asked me to wake her half an hour before she actually needed to get up for school, so she could "savor" the morning of her first day. "That's really weird, isn't it?" she asked me.

Yes, it was pretty weird, I told her.

"I didn't even know that could happen. How *could* that happen?"

I didn't know, I said. Maybe it was that we both were pretty anxious about her starting middle school.

That woke her up. "*You're* not supposed to be anxious. I'm the one who's going."

"Different anxieties," I said. "One situation, two sets of reactions." But I could see that it was dawning on her that she didn't quite like it, that it was as if I'd usurped her anxiety—usurped her dream?

"Yeah"—she was wide awake now, and frowning—"except that you were the one yelling in both of our dreams. And you were yelling about exactly the same thing." She got out of bed. "Matching dreams," she muttered as she left me sitting on her bed. "Weird." Her long, long, glossy-straight hair swung behind her.

I didn't call out to her to say that in fact our dreams didn't altogether match. I didn't even remember this until I was downstairs in the kitchen, making coffee, but in my dream, after I finished yelling at her, the scene shifted (the way it will in dreams, the way dreams are, says Hobson, "like psychosis") and I was with *my* mother, we were in Brooklyn, and she'd arranged a lunch date for us, with *my* childhood best friend, Susan, and her mother, Naomi. We were going to Lundy's, the lobster restaurant where my family always went for celebratory lunches when I was a child (so that even now lobster seems to me to define a celebration, though it's the rare celebration that involves lobster now, since neither my husband nor my daughter will eat it; they don't even like to look at it or smell it. And in Columbus, Ohio, it's insanely expensive, anyway. Even at my lavish fiftieth birthday party, I didn't have lobster; I made do with shrimp).

And Lundy's! I thought as I drank my coffee. Lundy's was closed for many years—it was boarded up, a ghost town of a giant restaurant—and when it finally reopened years ago, it wasn't the same (even if it had been the same, it wouldn't have been the same; it was so much a part of my childhood). After it reopened, I went there for lunch once with Grace and my friend Vicki—a high school friend with whom I'd recently become close again after twenty-five years of being out of contact—and her son, Silas, who was at the time *Grace's* best friend. The children were not quite three years old. We had a nice time but Vicki and I agreed that the restaurant wasn't anything like it had been "before."

Three years after that lunch at Lundy's, Vicki was dead. I'd never be able to think about Lundy's again without thinking of her.

On the morning that marked Grace's—and, five hundred miles away, Silas's—first day of sixth grade, five years had passed since Vicki's death.

In my dream, I was still so angry with Grace, I couldn't concentrate on the lunch that was ahead—and my mother kept trying to draw my attention back to it. We were walking on Sheepshead Bay Road, toward the restaurant on Emmons Avenue—my childhood neighborhood, the neighborhood I left the summer before (drum roll, please) I began sixth grade, the year Susan and I ceased to be best friends. Susan was about to start seventh grade then—just like Kristin was, on this day.

All those best friends! All those best friends and all those mothers.

I was confused, thinking about them all. Even *in* the dream, I was confused: was it Grace who was the child on the way to Lundy's, or was it me? And was the mother really my mother—or was *that* me? It seemed to me that both of us were me.

And then there was Grace's Kristin and my Susan—and Vicki, who had been the same sort of mother *I* was—the same sort of mother I *am*: expansive, extravagant, over-the-top, over-involved, unreserved. Vicki would have laughed about the five pairs of shoes. "How come only five?" she would have said. She would have understood about the hair appointment. She would have understood how anxious I was on this day; she would have worried aloud with me about whether I was right to keep Grace in this school, about whether there were other options I hadn't thought of. I missed her terribly. I always missed her, but at times like this—when something big was happening in Grace's life—I missed her especially. Our children's birthdays were just two days apart—Grace and Silas were practically twins, we used to say. We would compare notes about their milestones; we compared notes about the kinds of things that anyone else would have found boring. Vicki took everything that needed to be taken seriously about motherhood seriously, it seemed to me—and yet she was better than anyone at helping me to dismiss what needed dismissing, to laugh at what I should be laughing at—to see things clearly. Both she and I had waited a long time to have our children, and neither of us wanted to have more than one—one adored child. How devoted we were to them! How we loved them!

Half an hour later, on the way to school, I asked Grace if it didn't seem to her that I sometimes overdid things.

"Overdo them how?" she said. "Overdo what?"

"Everything. You know. Shoes. Food. Talk. Love."

"Well—yeah. Sure. You do everything in a big way."

"Right," I said. "I'm just wondering if I could learn to be a little more like Kristin's mother. A little more moderate. A little more cautious. Reserved."

Grace burst out laughing. "Sorry. It's just hard to imagine you like that," she said. "Would that even be you anymore?"

After I dropped her off and wished her luck—I was no longer allowed to kiss her goodbye; I hadn't been allowed to do that since the second grade—I thought about our matching dreams some more, about her making a mistake (the same mistake!) in both our dreams, and my flying off the handle. How she had probably taken me on as a symbolic representation of a part of herself—furious at herself, unforgiving, cruel—just as I had taken her on as a representation of a part of *my*self. Mirror image dreams.

And I was still thinking about Vicki—my mirror image, my perfect mother-friend, the one who always understood. Who had a little boy who was practically my daughter's twin. Who had to leave her baby, while I had gotten to stay.

Five years, I thought. She had already been gone for five years. It was hard to believe.

And I was startled—the number itself startled me. Five. Five pairs of shoes. Five weeks of withheld allowance. Five is how old children are when they start school.

Dreams pull in everything there *is* to pull in. You never know what you might find in them if you look around. *Until* you look around.

"You were really mad in that dream," Grace said again, that evening. She'd gotten through her first day of middle school. It was going to be a long three years, she could already tell. "I wonder if you were as mad at me in your dream as you were in mine."

"I was pretty mad."

"I've never seen you so mad in real life."

"In real life," I told her, "I'll never get that mad at you."

She raised one eyebrow at me. "How can you be so sure?"

Grace and I still tell each other our dreams, but I am careful not to overstay my welcome as a dream-teller. I choose among my dreams, reporting only the ones I believe may be of interest to her. No doubt she makes her own calculations about what to tell and what not to tell of the dreams she remembers. My mother and I exchange dreams too, but it isn't a fair trade, since she almost never remembers hers. To keep things more equitable, I don't tell her more than perhaps one dream a month. (It is always something of an event when she has one to tell, and because she remembers them so rarely, I suppose, the ones she does recall are always packed densely with meaning.)

I also have a friend with whom I exchange dreams—my closest friend, a poet. We have been friends for two decades, and we are as glad to hear each other's dreams (which we merrily pick apart as we talk on our cell phones while running errands or doing household chores) as we are to hear about the details of each other's waking lives—possibly gladder, since our lives (full of quarrels with spouses, complaints about colleagues, meals cooked, Netflix movies watched) are so much more mundane than our dreams.

But all of these—daughter, mother, best friend—are exceptions to the general rule that no one wants to hear anybody else's dreams, just as there are exceptions to the rule that *everyone* wants to talk about what he has dreamed. I know for a fact that this isn't true, that there are people who are disinclined to talk about their dreams even when they can remember them—which, most of the time, they can't, for those who are disinclined to tell tend to be those disinclined to tell even themselves. (This does not work in reverse—that is, those who usually don't remember their dreams seem no less inclined than anyone else to want to tell them when they do remember, and in fact may be even more likely than the rest of us to disregard the knowledge that most people have no desire to listen.)

I know this—that there are people who are not interested in talking about their dreams—because I am married to such a person. If my husband didn't talk in his sleep (indeed, shout and shriek and cry out in his sleep—evidently enacting his dreams: speaking—yelling—his own lines and pausing for the other speakers, whom only he can hear, to take their turns), I would never know what sort of dreams he has. And if it weren't for my occasionally reporting to him what I can glean from these lopsided, disjointed narratives, he himself would almost never know.

He is horrified when I tell him. He would prefer *not* to know. (And so I tell him only when I can't help myself—when what he seemed to be dreaming is just too interesting to *me* to keep quiet about.) Not long ago he dreamed of a barn, which someone was evidently demanding that he tear down ("No, I won't! That's a good barn! That would be a terrible thing to do! Why would you want to do that?"), and then I thought he must have been protesting the tearing down of a good fence as well, because he cried, "No, no, not the fence!"—and then, an instant later, he was calling for our dog, our real-life dog, Molly. He was screaming her name, and I thought the barn must have fallen on her, because then he began to croon to her, comforting her as she lay dying, I thought—I was listening closely, carefully, by then, fully awake and turned on my side, facing him, propped up on my elbow—or (I thought hopefully, as his tone shifted) calling her to him, softly, trying to distract her from whatever disaster was about to befall her. I thought there was a good chance it was the latter, because after he spoke her name softly a few times, he offered to scratch her neck the way she likes it, and then he became peaceful, the dream was over, and it hadn't left him shaken the way his dreams almost always do.

For once, hours later, when he woke up and we talked about it, he actually remembered at least part of his dream. He had no memory of the barn, whose or where it was or whom he'd been arguing with about it, but he remembered the fence, and Molly. Somehow the fence around our yard—which in real life he had put up himself just days before, replacing our old fence—came down, and Molly escaped from the yard, where she spends much of her real-life time, barking at anyone who passes through the alley behind the studio where my husband paints. In the dream the yard opened out onto a highway, and Molly ran into traffic.

"And what about the end, then?" I wanted to know. "Was she hit by a car? Were you holding her while she died? Or were you . . . I don't know, crouching by the side of the highway and calling to her, to get her to come to you, to get out of the path of oncoming traffic?"

But he didn't remember that part of the dream at all, and it was as if my questions had reminded him of what he really thought about dreams. "Why are you bothering me with this? It was just a dream. It's meaningless. A random firing of synapses." He refused to talk about it anymore. And the little we had talked about it had put him in a bad mood. Or the dream had. Or he'd been feeling bad to begin with—hence the dream—and hadn't known it (and perhaps still wouldn't have known it if I hadn't made him talk about what he had dreamed).

When he is awake, Glen is a man of few words, and so soft-spoken when he does speak that half the time I can't hear him. Grace and I are always asking him to repeat himself. He also speaks very slowly, with long pauses, and more often than not we will think he's finished when he isn't, and jump in. "What's the point of talking at all?" he'll say then. "You two don't even let me finish my sentences."

And Grace and I will say, in unison, "*What* did you say?"

She and I are the noisy ones. We both enjoy talking. We do quite a lot of it. And while I don't think either of us is particularly loud (I used to be, growing up, and had to make a conscious effort not to be; Grace isn't, by nature—but then *she* is not from New York), we do know how to *project*: no one has ever had any trouble hearing either one of us. I took drama and elocution lessons as a child in Brooklyn, and Grace has been acting on the stage since she was seven years old, so that even when she's feeling shy, she knows how to muster the effort not to seem so. She not only projects, but has excellent diction, even when she's going a mile a minute. (She and I both speak very rapidly—so rapidly that Glen will sometimes insist he can't understand a word we're saying, even though he can *hear* us well enough.) The point is: between the two of us, there is quite a lot of communicative *sound*, which has only served to make Glen quieter and quieter as the years have passed.

It could have gone the other way, I suppose: it might have forced him to raise his voice. Instead, he has practically given up talking altogether. He can go days without uttering more than a few words. When I mention this, he tells me he has never felt a pressing need to express himself *in* words.

But asleep—asleep, everything is different for him. As I say, he doesn't just talk in his sleep, he *roars* in his sleep; he bellows in his sleep. For years, nearly every night, he argued that "the boat" was his ("I *bought* the boat, I *paid* for the boat, it's *my* boat, it's not *your* boat")—but I never knew who was trying to take the boat away, or why. Listening to Glen sleep is like listening in on one side of a telephone conversation, but harder to follow—like a television show you catch bits of as you're flipping through the channels, because there is also action I'm not seeing, both during the pauses for the other speaker *and* while he is protesting, scolding, threatening, raging—not to mention that the leaps in the action are impossible to make sense of because, after all, this is a dream, not a television show.

He never dreams about the boat anymore, at least not out loud. And he has no memory—he has never had any memory, not even on the morning after one of them—of the dreams about the boat.

My very first conversation with Glen (he will deny it; he will claim to have no memory of it—and I will believe him, because he remembers *nothing*; his dreams are the least of what he doesn't remember) was about dreams. This was the first time I heard him use the phrase "a random firing of synapses."

It was a public conversation. It was when he was a student in a writing workshop I was teaching, many years ago. (I hasten to say that we didn't start dating until a year after the class ended. The question of why I would have *started* dating someone who I knew disbelieved in the meaningfulness of dreams may be worth pursuing, but I won't even begin to go down that road here.) The class, in those days before we had an MFA program of our own, with separate workshops for advanced undergraduates and creative writing MFAs, was made up mostly of graduate students in English, with a few junior and senior English majors and a couple of graduate students from other departments. Glen was an MFA student in painting. The class had been talking about the use of dreams in stories: how much is too much, whether some of the students had been relying on their characters' dreams to do too much of the work of the story, whether dreams in fiction should be avoided altogether—"It's just too obviously a *device*," someone said, and someone else said, "They just slow down the action," and I'm almost sure someone said, "Who wants to hear about a character's dreams, anyway? How boring is that?" Someone who had taken too many workshops said, "Isn't reporting a dream more like telling than showing, really, though it *looks* like showing?" But until Glen spoke (and it was the first time he'd spoken, weeks into the course; it was the only time he ever *volunteered* to speak), no one had considered the possibility he raised: that dreams could tell us nothing about a character, that they were merely (to put Hobson's words into my future husband's mouth) cognitive trash. Mental noise. Random firings.

The other students looked at one another, and at me, and went silent. It was as if one of them had said that evolution was a hoax. They looked relieved when I laughed. "Right," I said. "Absolutely. We can all agree that dreams have no meaning."

"They don't," he said.

Was he kidding? He didn't seem to be. He seemed puzzled by my assumption that he was. What followed was the kind of "argument" (let's call it a lively discussion) that I like to think marks my teaching style. I enjoy being disagreed with in the classroom; I like a good lively discussion.

It's diagnostic of my marriage that eighteen years later I still don't know if he meant what he said, or if he means it when he says it now. I think he might half-mean it; I think he would *like* to believe it, because his own dreams, from the evidence overheard, are so disturbing. (Then again, it's possible that he has "good" dreams, too, but that when he does, he doesn't have them out loud. How would I ever know? How would *he* ever know?)

Here's another thing I think: that even though he remembers little or nothing of his dreams, and wishes I wouldn't tell him what I know about them—and quickly shuts down the conversation when I can't help myself and tell him anyway—he must want me to know what he's been dreaming. Unconsciously want it, I mean. Otherwise he'd *be* quieter about it in his sleep, wouldn't he?

I don't say this to him. I wouldn't dare. I say it to our daughter, though. She has been listening to him dream aloud her whole life, so what he says in his sleep—the fact that he says anything in his sleep—has from time to time inevitably been a subject of our conversation. And because Glen often paints all night and then sleeps during the day, sometimes Grace and I—hearing him shouting or screaming—will find ourselves drawn to the same spot in the upstairs hallway, she emerging from her room, I from my study, to stand together on the other side of my closed bedroom door.

"I don't know," she says when I ask my question. "Maybe he just *has* to be loud when he's asleep. To make up for being so quiet when he's awake, you know? To make up for all the things he doesn't say."

My husband (or, perhaps I should say, my husband's *claims*) aside, most of us find our own dreams fascinating. And the more convoluted and mysterious our dreams, the harder they are to follow and parse, the more fascinated we seem to be by them—and the more we want to talk about them. But there's hardly anything drearier to listen to than a recitation of the puzzle pieces that make up someone else's complicated dream ("I was standing in water up to my knees, and then I was in a house. I think it might have been the house I grew up in . . . oh, yes, it was, because there was my mother and my younger sister, but they looked the way they do now . . . and that house was torn down years ago to make way for a shopping mall. . . . Anyway, I was in the living room, and then suddenly it wasn't the living room anymore, it was more like a basement, but with some of the characteristics of my old living room—the couch, the matching loveseat, the big painting of the sunset. And then my next-door neighbor—no, not from then, from now. You know Bill Klein, don't you? One house south of mine? Well, it doesn't matter—Bill walked in, and he was carrying this enormous chocolate cake. . . .").

It may be, in fact, that the level of interest anyone else is likely to have in what we have dreamed is inversely proportional to the level of interest *we* have in it. Because the truth is that I can't think of anything that is as compelling as a dream is to the person who has dreamed it that is *at the same time* so devoid of interest to others. Bad art comes close: a poem an undergraduate writes with which he's entranced, and which he can't wait to put into the hands of everyone he knows (or, better yet, to read aloud at an open mic night, so that his audience will expand to other poetry lovers who are as yet strangers to him)—but which is nothing but a jumble of entirely personal or otherwise obscure references, abstractions, generalizations, and clichés. All of the meaning—so clear and urgent for the bad poet—is missing (as is the beauty, so obvious to him) for his audience. But in such a case it's plain to us that the writer is kidding himself, poor thing. He isn't seeing the poem clearly; he only *thinks* he's written something meaningful and beautiful (what's valuable about it—what *could* be valuable about it—is still locked away inside him; it hasn't made it to the page). With a dream, nobody's kidding himself. Nobody's kidding anybody. It really *is* interesting, both meaningful and beautifully made, if you're the one dreaming it.

And dreams themselves—and just the fact that we do dream, and the way our minds *make* dreams—are so interesting, it's strange, really, that the particular details of any one dream should be so tedious. But just as in a bad poem, the tedium has something to do with what's missing. Everything is so loaded (indeed, laden) with meaning in a dream—but if you aren't the one whose sleeping self devised those signs and symbols—those vivid places and events and characters who morph into other characters and slip through time and space—there's nothing to the dream at all but a set of random, incoherent happenings and images. The meaning that the dreamer (like the bad poet) attaches to every detail of a dream, even if she can't put her finger on what those meanings are (oh, but she feels them! *everything* in the dream resonates with hidden meaning), is not only obscure, it's of no interest to her audience. *Who cares?* you want to say but politely don't.

Writing about dreams, which I have wanted to do for a long time (because my own dreams are so interesting to me, of course) is—it should go without saying, then—a bad idea. Which is why, for a long time, I resisted the impulse. If nobody wants to hear about anyone else's dreams, why would anybody want to read about them?

(I do not exempt myself from this *nobody/anybody*, either. As I began to think seriously about [finally] writing this, one of the ideas I had was to collect other people's dreams. I was especially interested in recurring dreams, I told my friends—and acquaintances, and family and colleagues and students. I asked everyone I knew to e-mail me their dreams, and I collected hundreds of them over a period of months. But I could not get myself to sit down and read through them as the e-mails came in. Instead, I saved them. I created a special, separate mailbox to transfer them to: *dream responses*. As each new response came in, I moved it from my inbox to my dream-response box without reading it. And for the longest time I didn't even want to copy-paste the dreams from the e-mails in my special mailbox into a word processing document—it was too boring even to *look* at them. Finally I did, though. I copy-pasted all the dreams into a new Word document—*other people's dreams*, I called it—and periodically I would square my shoulders and open the document and start to read. But after just the first few sentences my eyes would glaze over, then begin to droop closed, and suddenly I was too sleepy to continue working and I would find myself standing up, drifting away from the computer, out of my study, into my bedroom, to lie down for a little while before I could go back to work. And once I *did* get back to work, I knew better than to start reading the *dreams* file again. I would work on something else—anything else—instead. It was the only way I could be sure I would stay awake long enough to get anything done at all.)

I used to think that no one wanted to hear anyone else's dreams because we—dreamers and listeners both—are so self-centered. We are so enamored of our own mysteries, and so impatient about the private mysteries of others (except, perhaps, when we have first fallen in love, and everything about the beloved is of great interest, his mysteries in particular). We generally don't want evidence that the people we know are deeper and stranger than they seem to be. We might not mind hearing their secrets (especially if they are juicy ones we aren't supposed to tell to anyone else—affairs, hidden resentments, skeletons in the closet), but we don't want to hear secrets in code, things we'd have to think too hard about, things we'd be unlikely to understand even if we did think very hard about them.

But I'm not so sure about this anymore. After I finally forced myself to stay awake and read through all the dreams I had collected, and began also to listen more closely, and patiently, when anyone told me a dream (always, when rendered aloud—even by the most gifted storytellers among us—recited exactly the way a child will tell the plot of a movie: "And then I turned the corner—or, no, it wasn't a corner, it was a sort of platform I had to step onto, and then I saw my uncle—no, wait, not my uncle, my brother. But before *that*, my brother or my uncle—or maybe it was someone else altogether—

was looking out a window. Oh, and then there was a fire. . . .”), I figured something out that I can’t believe I hadn’t been able to see before.

The reason we dislike hearing other people’s dreams, I think, is much less damning and less complicated than I’d been assuming: it’s mostly just a matter of *story*, and the lack of it.

Because we love stories. Even those of us (that would be me) who aren’t particularly storycentric—who insist we prefer the *why* to the *what* or the *how*—are constantly, automatically, making narratives. It’s human nature to turn everything we do and everything that happens to us into little narratives. When we tell each other, over dinner, about our days—or tell each other about our childhoods, or about a failed marriage, or about that job we quit, or about last night’s blind date—we turn the recitation into a story, or a series of stories.

But dreams don’t tell stories. They are misshapen and rambling and artless and ragged and disconnected. Dreams don’t care about graceful form, or about plot—about events that are linked logically, and in which one thing leads to another—and they don’t care about motivation (not in the sense that we understand motivation in our conscious lives) or about characters being consistent. Dreams may unspool each night like movies, or novels—*full* of characters, rich in setting, with plenty of action and plenty of feeling—but they aren’t really a bit like movies or novels: they don’t hold their shape; they hardly *have* a shape. They are, in fact, just like life before we make our narratives out of it—before we shape it and divide it up into manageable, interpretable, communicable, coherent bits.

If a dream has meaning to its dreamer, it’s because the dreamer knows how it felt to be *in* the dream, knows how the dream made her feel both while it was unfolding and afterward. She alone knows the context for everything that transpired and everything and everyone that made an appearance. Even if she isn’t consciously, actively analyzing the parts of the dream once she’s awake and going about her business, she can *feel* there is more to the dream than its telling would suggest.

A dream has a readership, a viewership, of one. Its only purpose is to communicate to that audience. It doesn’t want to be told to others; it wasn’t made to be told to others. It resists telling, every bit as much as the listener resists listening.

And we human beings are so contrary and so stubborn! We insist on telling it anyway. Just as the dream tells us, insistently, *Listen! I have something important to say!*, we say, *Listen! Listen to this dream I had!*

Because we cannot keep a secret. Because we cannot resist the urge to repeat something fascinating we have been told. It is as if we are gossiping about ourselves.

5

One always feels, waking from a dream, as if one *has* been "told" something. Even when the message is difficult to understand; even when it seems to have been written in an unfamiliar or barely remembered, once-known language, or in an indecipherable hand; even when the message is fragmentary (even when no more than one small, torn piece of it remains), or the memory of having received it is so fragile its receiver wonders if she had received it (*did I only dream that I had dreamed?*); even when the dreamer, waking, skeptical, resolutely shakes off the sense that some important information has been conveyed — telling herself that she is mistaken, that her *sense* is not to be trusted — the dreamer wakes with the unmistakable impression, however fleeting, that a message has been received. (The sleep scientists would argue, I imagine, that this represents a sort of category error — something on the order of doodles that only at first glance appear to be sentences of narrative prose.)

Whether a dream's message is as easy to interpret as turning the knob on an unlocked door (or — for me, sometimes — peering in through an open, doorless doorway), or so difficult that the unbolting would appear to require the skills of a master locksmith, the *opportunity* for access it offers to our unconscious minds is unparalleled. Even when access is blocked — even when we cannot unlock the door, when we rattle the doorknob and pick at the lock and pull pin after pin and still the door remains securely closed — when all we can do is marvel at the complexities and strength of the lock itself — I have no doubt that behind that door there are rooms of which our waking selves are unaware, and through which, if only we keep trying (I think of the characters in old movies, touching everything in sight in their determination to open up the secret passageway they just know "is here somewhere"), we have the potential to walk.

Where it seems to me the sleep and dream scientists have done their most useful work is in their attempting to unlock the secret not of what it means *that* we dream—and certainly not of the meaning of our dreams themselves, which for the most part they simply deny—but of how dreams are made at all.

Here's what they have figured out (or theorized, at least) so far:

When we sleep, the brain closes its door to the world outside it—the outside world, what I've been calling the "real" world. With that door closed, outside information can't get in nearly as easily as it does while we are awake (although I am guessing that some of us have flimsier doors to the outside than others do—since my husband and my daughter, in sleep, are both able to shut out outside information completely, so that nothing short of shaking them or shouting directly into their ears will wake them, while I sleep so lightly that information streams in all night long: I wake at a whisper, a breath, a click). Once the "door" shuts—steel or hollow-core, securely or lightly—the brain "self-activates" (this is the term researchers use). This self-activation changes the brain's chemical climate, and among the changes is the shutting off of the two chemical systems that are necessary for waking-world consciousness.

Although the various autonomic, or self-regulating, mechanisms of our bodies are still taking place—the kinds of physiological changes or movements that don't depend on our volition, such as penile erection and minute facial and eye movements—beyond these primitive, spontaneous activities, in which the brain operates on its most basic level, brain work when we sleep is different physiologically than it is when we're awake: it is as if the brain operates on a different track altogether than its waking track.

The theory is that chemical activity (or, rather, the lack of certain kinds of chemical activity) determines the differences between the waking and dreaming tracks. The question of why we require two such tracks is what keeps psychoanalysis and biology standing glaring at each other from opposite sides of the room (and art sides with psychoanalysis, so that biology sometimes complains about being unfairly outnumbered). At the most drastic reaches of the argument, there are the researchers who believe that rapid eye movement (REM) sleep—the periodic, rapid, jerky movement of the eyeballs under the lids during certain periods of sleep, which for over five decades has been widely accepted as the stage of sleep in which dreaming occurs — has in fact *no* relationship to our ability to dream (and, to be sure, there *is* research that shows that we can be in REM sleep without dreaming and that we can dream without being in REM). At the other end of the spectrum, there is Hobson's belief that REM itself controls dream images and narratives (a dream of flying, for example, would be caused, according to Hobson, by the uprolling of the eyeballs during REM). If dreams reflect psychological concerns, Hobson says, it's because the cortex tries to make sense of the random neuronal activity instigated by signals shooting up from the brain stem to the visual cortex and other parts of the forebrain. Rather grudgingly, he suggests that this — the interpretation — *may* reveal something of the dreamer's psychological state.

REM was discovered in the early fifties, and by some accounts only by accident. Eugene Aserinsky was a graduate student in physiology at the University of Chicago, and according to Hobson his interest was in studying attention in children. When the children he was working with got bored, they would get sleepy and their eyes would begin to close; therefore, he put electrodes near their eyes (Hobson neglects to explain the "therefore," but implies — and never pauses to wonder at this — that he means "to keep the children awake"). Aserinsky was surprised to discover that when the tired, bored children fell asleep anyway, their eyes darted back and forth and up and down behind their closed eyelids. (Other accounts have Aserinsky *trying* to connect eye movement and brain activity, and experimenting on his own son, whom he'd hooked up to an ancient — even in 1951 — brain-wave machine, something called an Offner Dynograph. In this version of the story, he and his son both fought sleep as the night wore on, and as the father nodded and tried not to doze over his machine, he suddenly noticed that the pens tracking his son's eye movements, as well as the pens registering brain activity, were swinging from side to side, suggesting that the boy, Armond, was alert and looking around in the other room. When he went in to check on Armond — expecting to find him wide awake — he discovered that he was fast asleep, and thus stumbled upon REM. Still other accounts suggest that Aserinsky was actively investigating eye movement in sleep, using his son as a guinea pig — but all accounts accept him as the father of REM, as well as of poor Armond, eight years old at the time of his father's crucial discovery.)

Aserinsky and his dissertation advisor, Nathaniel Kleitman, published a two-page paper in the journal *Science* in September 1953. An article by Chip Brown in *Smithsonian* magazine, on the fiftieth anniversary of the publication of Aserinsky and Kleitman's research, describes the paper as "a fine example of the maxim that the eye can see only what the mind knows," pointing out that "for thousands of years the physical clues of REM sleep were baldly visible to anyone who ever gazed at the eyelids of a napping child or studied the twitching paws of a sleeping dog," and that "the association of a certain stage of sleep with dreaming might have been described by any number of observant cave men; in fact, if the 17,000-year-old Lascaux cave painting of a presumably dreaming Cro-Magnon hunter with an erect penis is any indication, maybe it was."

At all events, the discovery of REM launched a new branch of medicine, leading to the diagnosis and treatment of sleep disorders, and, says Chip Brown, "shifted scientists' focus from the dreaming person to the dreaming brain, [inspiring] new models in which the chimerical dramas of the night were said to reflect random neural fireworks rather than the hidden intentions of unconscious conflict or the escapades of disembodied souls." Aserinsky's discovery of REM thus "underscored the view that the 'self' is not a fixed state but reflects fluctuating brain chemistry and electrical activity."

By now we know that REM sleep occurs regularly, and that the brain enters REM four or five times a night, at roughly ninety-minute intervals, each period lasting about twenty minutes. Michel Jouvet, in 1962, proposed that REM is generated in the pontine brain stem (or "pons"), which produces waves of excitation to which eye muscles respond; he suggested that REM sleep exhibits two other properties as a result of signals received from the pons: a low level of brain activity and an inhibition of muscle tone. The pons also excites the thalamus (which contains numerous structures for cognition), which, in turn, excites the cortex: the cortex misinterprets the thalamus's signal, treating it as if it were actually seen or heard.

During the early days of sleep research, which Hobson defines as the period from 1953, when Aserinsky first published his REM findings, through 1975, the focus was on establishing correlations between the narratives that unspool in dreams — their "plots" — as reported by dreamers, and autonomic mechanisms as recorded by electroencephalogram (EEG) or polygraphs (lie detectors). The extant theory was that "the eye movements of REM sleep could be predicted from the sequence of directional changes in the dreamer's 'hallucinated gaze,'" says Hobson. This turned out not to be true, and Hobson notes that the failure of this theory was, in retrospect, not very surprising, because no correlations between "peripheral physiology" and emotion have ever been found — not even when people are awake.

More recent sleep and dream research has concerned itself less with brain chemistry or REM than with questions about *who* (or what) dreams — do animals? babies? fetuses? — and about the usefulness of dreaming, and indeed of sleeping itself.

The first set of these questions seems to be much easier to answer than the second. Animals and babies *do* dream — at least, it looks like they do, by the only measures available to determine whether dreaming occurs, in situations in which we can't get direct reports. Both animals and babies exhibit REM and brain activation in sleep (as do fetuses, once they've reached thirty weeks). In fact, the very young — babies, puppies, kittens — exhibit considerably more brain activation in sleep than adults do, according to Hobson, who points out that this means that "a brain substrate for dreaming is present at birth," although he also suggests that this particular line of research gets us nowhere, since without language, the subjective experience of a dream can't be the same as that of adult humans. Researchers who study dreaming in children report that children begin to offer such subjective accounts of their dreams at about age three, when they acquire both language and "propositional" (or symbolic) thought; the assumption is that until (or unless) the language to express dream content is available, dreaming doesn't "count" as dreaming at all. (My own adult experience of children's dreams — my daughter's reporting of hers — suggests that dreaming that "counts" as dreaming can begin earlier than three: Grace was reporting her dreams to me before she was two, and more than thirteen years later she still remembers the most disturbing of them.) At all events, the question of whether dreaming is a meaningful activity before it can be reported to others (or, in the case of animals, when it can*not* be reported — or at least not to us) strikes me as worth exploring, as is the question of how memories are formed before the acquisition of language. It surprises (indeed, confounds) me that it has not been. (But to consider it here would take me so far afield of dreaming that I daren't begin. I'll say this, however: I have a small store of memories from well before the age of three; my daughter seems to have a much larger store—and because she has me to test them against, we know that her visual memories are quite accurate; and my closest friend—the poet—has at least one clear visual memory that dates back to her early infancy. I'm convinced, too, that some of these earliest stored memories make their way into dreams, whether we have access to them when we are awake or not. Freud believed this, too. In *The Interpretation of Dreams* he noted that in our dreams we "have at [our] command memories which are inaccessible in waking life." Indeed, the meaning of pre-language-acquisition memories *and* dreams—which sidestep language and make use of symbols at what seems to be a very primitive level—seems to so warrant serious exploration that the very thought of it makes me wish I could have pursued a second life, devoted to memory/cognition/language-acquisition research.)

A great deal is now known about who and what dreams, how often, and for how long. Michel Jouvet has reported ultradian (several times a day) periodicity of dreams for various species: for rats, dreaming occurs every ten minutes; for cats, every twenty-five minutes; for elephants, every one hundred and eighty minutes. The average duration of each dream (each episode of dreaming) is also species-specific: for rats, two minutes; for cats, five minutes; for birds, five to fifteen seconds, depending on the bird species. Human beings dream five times a night, twenty minutes at a time. Chimpanzees spend almost as much time dreaming as we do (they dream for ninety minutes each night, as opposed to our hundred) and cats dream twice as much—something that will probably not come as a surprise to cat owners, since cats are always sleeping, and so much of their sleep is marked by twitching and other kinds of easily observable movement that suggests dream activity.

We still don't know if fish, amphibians, or reptiles dream (there is no way to measure dreaming in these creatures, Jouvet says)—or if dolphins do (and Jouvet cautions us to be careful not to make assumptions—dolphins are smart; therefore, they must dream—for we can see from the results of research already done that brain complexity is not the criterion for dreaming). It was believed for decades that only mammals experienced REM sleep; recent research on zebra finches implanted with EEG electrodes disproved that, and the general assumption now is that all warm-blooded animals dream.

The question of what sleep and dreams are *for*, despite all the research that has been undertaken, appears to be unanswerable. Curiously enough, even though sleep scientists have focused exclusively on the physiological need for dreaming, there is no real consensus on what that need might actually be. Hobson's theory (*one* of Hobson's theories, the relevant one at this juncture) is that dreams exist to remind us that we have the capacity to move — so that each night we are "born again" with a sense of fictitious movement. But then Hobson also believes (as I said many pages ago) that sleep itself is necessary because it refreshes our skills each night (by activating our brains).

The truth is that although everybody knows that sleep is necessary (one doesn't have to look very far for advice about how much sleep we need, how to get more sleep, how we *must* get more sleep) and we have some idea what happens — or at least what the result of "what happens" is — when we *don't* sleep (studies have shown that sleep deprivation impairs drivers at least as much as drunkenness, and that people who don't get sufficient sleep are more likely to make mistakes of all kinds than the well-rested will), nobody really knows what happens when we do.

Robert Stickgold, a cognitive neuroscientist at Harvard, joked to a *Slate* reporter interviewing him that "the function of sleep is to cure sleepiness." In fact, the theory of sleep that he pursues in his work is that we sleep in order to boost our capacity to remember and to learn. The evidence for this, he says, comes from behavioral research. In an experiment Stickgold and his colleagues published in 2000, for instance, subjects were asked to identify the orientation of diagonal bars against a background of horizontal bars. For the most part, people who returned for re-testing later the same day showed little improvement, while those who returned to be re-tested after a night of sleep did significantly better — and the improved scores of the sleepers were proportional to the amount of slow-wave (a stage of non-REM) sleep they had gotten early in the night and the amount of REM sleep they had gotten late in the night. Furthermore, when subjects were deprived of sleep the night after learning the task, their performance did not improve later, even after two subsequent nights of sleep. The conclusion: sleep within thirty hours of learning a new task is required for improved performance.

There are plenty of other studies that show evidence of a link between learning or memory and some portion of sleep. A 2004 German study took the question further—into problem- or puzzle-solving—by having subjects work on a series of related math problems that contained a hidden rule that, once discovered, would enable the problem-solver to work out solutions to individual problems faster. Subjects who were allowed a night's sleep before they returned to the problems uncovered the shortcut twice as often as those who had stayed awake, and the researchers concluded that the "flash of insight" experienced by the sleepers was the result of the "restructuring of representations in memory" during sleep. Even more recent studies from Stickgold's lab suggest that sleep helps people make sense of information they received during the day: people given lists of related words did better at describing what it was that the words had in common after they'd slept.

Stickgold believes that sleep's function in "stabilizing and shaping" memories, and integrating new memories into older ones, may explain the role of sleep in evolution, providing an adaptive advantage to make up for the fact that animals can't hunt for food or produce offspring and are more vulnerable to predators when they're asleep—otherwise, why *would* sleep have been kept in our arsenal of behaviors? Michel Jouvet ponders this, too. He points out that dreaming seems downright dangerous for animals (when they dream, they are essentially paralyzed, and the ordinary sleep-to-waking threshold is increased), so how, he wonders, *can* it provide an evolutionary advantage? He confesses that this is one of the great mysteries of his research.

In 1983, Francis Crick (of the famous Watson and Crick, who cracked the DNA code in 1959) proposed that the function of dreams was to "clear the circuits" of the brain so that there would be space to register the next day's events (a simpler theory than most; perhaps Crick had run out of complicated theories by the eighties). His explanation satisfied no one, and the evolutionary role of sleeping and dreaming continues to be endlessly speculated about and elaborated upon by sleep scientists. Franklin and Zyphur, in "The Role of Dreams in the Evolution of the Human Mind," note that the advantage of rehearsing threatening situations in dreams is clear—but that for the "rehearsals" to work ("in order for this dream mechanism to be selected for"), a crucial aspect of evolutionary selection would be that "the perceived threats encountered during a dream must be experienced as real" (because think how evolutionarily disadvantageous it would be to come across a threatening scenario in real life and invest the time required to wonder whether or not what's happening is real). Thus, "certain higher-order mental processes, which would function to appraise the situation in an intellectual fashion (mostly frontal areas), would likely have to be deactivated," Franklin and Zyphur conclude (and indeed this deactivation is indicated by research by Hobson and others). They even offer an evolutionary explanation for "good dreams"—since "in terms of pure survival value, those individuals who best interact with those around them, i.e., those who interact without interpersonal conflict and confrontation, will likely have better access to resources in their social group, be it mates or food," and so practicing not only for threats but for ordinary social interactions would be quite reasonably selected for.

The latest research (as of June 2009), by Matthew Walker and his colleagues at the University of California, Berkeley, focuses on how sleep, and specifically REM sleep, influences our ability to read emotions in other people's faces. After a sixty- or ninety-minute nap, or without any nap, Walker's subjects were asked to interpret the facial expressions of people in photographs. In this small study (Walker worked with just thirty-six adults), he found that those who'd experienced REM sleep during a nap were better able to identify expressions of "positive emotions" such as happiness; those who didn't sleep long enough to achieve REM sleep—or did not have the chance to sleep at all—were actually better able to interpret such "negative expressions" as anger and fear. Walker's conclusion, reported at the annual meeting of the Associated Professional Sleep Societies (and described in *Time* magazine), was that one function of REM sleep, then, may be to "allow the brain to sift through that day's events, process any negative emotion attached to them, then strip it away from the memories." REM sleep, Walker suggests, offers a "nocturnal soothing balm," the purpose of which is to try "to ameliorate the sharp emotional chips and dents that life gives you." He detects an evolutionary advantage in this: "If you're walking through the jungle and you're tired, it might benefit you more to be hypersensitive to negative things," whereas when you're well-rested and thus more likely to be sensitive to positive signals, you'll do better at tasks that provide "some kind of reward," such as locating food . . . or "a wife."

All of this, I admit, sounds sensible enough (if a little obvious), so what I am left to wonder about is why any of it precludes the notion that dreams themselves are meaningful—not "impersonal necessities forced on the brain by nature," in the words of the polymath Piero Scaruffi, who approvingly boils down Hobson's and other researchers' work in this way. That the sleep scientists (and their cheerleaders) are so determinedly committed to the role of "impersonal necessities"—chemistry, physiology, neurobiology—when it comes to the making of dreams, and set themselves up in such fervent opposition to psychoanalytic theory, which (they complain) ignores *how* dreams are made by our brains and pays attention only to what our dreams are about and what we make of what they are about, means that there is no one trying to look at the big picture (the big sleep?). Like most academic battles, the question of dreams becomes . . . well, academic.

To understand dreaming in a way that will be useful (which is to say, meaningful) to us as human beings trying to make sense of ourselves, it seems to me self-evident that we need to look at every aspect of dreaming from every angle. But who will do this? I may be kidding myself, imagining that someone will.

Of course, that is what I am trying to do—to *begin* to do—in this essay. But I don't have all the angles. All I've got is my own. This is both the curse and the thrill of the personal essay—it defines both the essayist's limits and limitlessness. That is, all I know is what I know, and while I can (and do) write myself blue in the face about all that I know—indeed, what I know better than anyone: my life, myself—there is so much more that I don't know at all, and everything I write serves to remind me of this.

In middle age I have somehow become the sort of writer who wanders into unfamiliar territory—disciplines I only *wish* I had a solid grounding in—and the sort of reader who reads to become, if not an expert, then at least a repository of the thoughts of others (properly educated, trained, skilled, *expert* others). While I may not (I don't) always want to know how *things* work (I don't mind at all not knowing how the internal combustion engine operates; I have no desire to take my computer apart and put it back together, and when technical support consists of someone telling me to do just that, I demand to talk to a supervisor), I always want to know how *we* work. All my life I've wanted this, I realize; it is only how much I think I have to know in order to know this that's changed—and the kinds of things I now know I need to know.

I am very glad, for example, to know the science behind the making of dreams, about which I'd known nothing, not even that there was a research field *of* sleep and dream science, but it puzzles me that so little effort (I am being polite: no effort at all) has been made to link science and psychoanalysis—which is to say, science and art. Even the brilliant scientist and writer Douglas Hofstadter, who is thoroughly engaging on the subjects of thought, consciousness, and creativity, dismisses dreams as "random meandering." How can this be? *Why* can this be?

How I wish that more were known—that more were contemplated—about the intersection of biology and experience and circumstance, physiology and culture and imagination. I wish—I suppose this is really what I mean to say—that the science of the mind and the art of the mind weren't always positioned as antithetical, that the "experts" believed it possible to appreciate—to be awestruck by, even to accept the impenetrable complexity of—the mysteries of the mind *and* to plumb them at the same time.

It's not answers I'm looking for so much as better questions.

Even the psychoanalytically inclined cannot seem to resist the temptation to try to reduce the complexities to manageable bits. We speak—*I* speak—of "interpreting" dreams, as if they required mediative explication, as if they really did come to us each night in a foreign language, and making sense of them involved translation, line by painstaking line. But understanding one's own dreams is more like reading Wallace Stevens—or looking at a painting of Mark Rothko's—than it is like the one-to-one correlation (no matter how graceful, how beautiful, or even how liberal that correlation) of translation. To make "sense" of our dreams, we don't interpret them so much as we feel our way through them; one thing leads to the next—away from the dream, then back toward it, then away again—and we follow where our feelings and associations lead us. If dream interpretation can be thought of as a matter of translation, then it's *homophonic* translation we're after: based not on a knowledge of the foreign language in which the original was "written," but on the sound of it—what each sound reminds us of, what it makes us think about, how it makes us feel.

And thus the interpretation of a dream, like the interpretation of a work of art, is layered, variable, fluid. If there is such a thing as a wholly incorrect interpretation, then it will come about only when the dream—like the work of art—has been treated as if it were beside the point, when it has been set aside in favor of what the interpreter wants to find there, rather than what is being offered.

But if a dream is like a work of art, then perhaps the better analogy to interpreting it is the making *of* art, from first draft (first strokes, first notes, first shapes) to finished piece, not the experience of art made by another. The artist's work in the beginning is like the mind at work in sleep: what is outside the self is quieted—shut out—as the artist "self-activates" in order to give form to what until then had been formless. It's only then that it can be "made sense of," that it can be shaped and further contemplated, shifted and responded to and re-responded to, until the ineffable has become expressible, until it can be communicated.

For that—for the shaping and remaking of what began spontaneously, for its essential nature to be seeable—we have to be awake.

6

The psychoanalyst Karen Horney considered dreams an attempt to solve conflicts, warning us, however, that the "solutions" our dreams provide were not likely to be healthy ones. For Horney, the main purpose of dreaming is to help us see what our conflicts *are*. In a lecture at the American Institute for Psychoanalysis in the 1950s, she told her audience of analysts in training, "We can interpret many dreams as though the real self of the dreamer were saying to him, 'Look how you despise yourself! Look what you are doing to yourself, how you are divided, what phantoms you are chasing, what a crooked path you are following, what a foul compromise you are trying to make!'"

That we would not be able to resolve conflicts in our sleep is no surprise. Why *would* dreams offer psychologically healthy solutions? (If we're not able to access such "health" while awake, I don't know why our sleeping selves would be more constructive, or wiser—especially given what we now know about brain chemistry.) Dreams, like poems, take the elements of what we're "looking at"—what's preoccupying, or troubling us (the conflict, Horney would call it)—and linger on and explore them: *here's what they are, here's what this is*, our dreams say—and *here's another way, and another way, to see it*.

That dreams are thus more like lyric than narrative poems is no surprise, either: we have to work hard to impose order on our feelings and even on our thoughts. When we're asleep (when the chemicals that help us keep things orderly are absent), our minds are free to roam and stop and stare, to link apparently (*waking*-apparently) unrelated images and ideas, to transform them, to walk us through the tumbling chaos of unordered thought and feeling so that we can just experience it—not ratiocinate around it, as we do when we are awake (awake and not creating).

If our sleeping minds reach for metaphors that make private sense to us and spin them in some new way (the variations in my dreams of rooms, caged animals, my grandparents)—just as a poet or a painter will return again and again to particular imagery, or a novelist or film-maker will return again and again to certain situations or types of characters or relationships—allowing us to wander among our own thoughts and feelings, it is when we are awake that this wandering becomes "of use." I'm interested in both the way we stockpile symbols (or signs, as Jung would have it) and make use of them in dream narratives *and* how we think about their meaning once we are awake, how much *give* there is (how personal, how specific, from one dreamer to the next) in our dreams.

A former student of mine—one of the many who responded to my request for recurring dreams—told me about what she called her "messiah baby dreams," taking pains to say that she was "not raised with any religion at all" and has never been religious, so the "sort of religious quality of these dreams has always bothered" her.

> *The specific details such as time, place, circumstances are each different, but what remains the same is this: I am hunted by someone that I never see or know the name of, and I know that this person is surrounded by the majority of the people who feel that my baby is dangerous. I have a small group of people that will try to protect me, but I never know who they are, and I also never know the father of my baby. This last part is significant because it is never something as horrible as my being raped and not knowing the father; it is more that I don't know how I have the baby.*

It was interesting to me that she called these dreams "religious," and interesting too that she didn't contextualize that designation for me: she assumed I'd know why she thought of them this way. And I guess I do, though I had to think about it. I'm guessing that she meant that there was something godlike in the important person whom she never sees or can name but who is "surrounded by the majority" who believe her baby to be dangerous, that being the mother of a baby of mysterious provenance made her think of Mary and Jesus, and that the group of people she knew she could count on (without knowing who they were) seemed to be disciples (though it's she, not the baby, they are hoping to protect). Still, I knew that if *I* had had a dream that made use of these narrative elements, I wouldn't have thought of them as "religious"; it made me wonder what she'd meant when she'd said she'd been raised without religion.

I don't know her well enough to know why she filled in the blanks in the way she did—or why she would be so disquieted by having done so. But I was struck by the sense of self-sacrifice and the emphasis she put on the idea of being "hunted" in the dream—in every version of the dream:

> *I am always hunted and . . . trying to find my way out of a country with my baby. I don't care if I die. I want the child to live and be safe. [And] it always ends with me being surrounded by a group of men who are about to take the baby away.*

It's unsettling, really, hearing the dreams of people you don't know very well—or rather, people you know as their ordinary, waking selves, but about whom you don't know very much of significance: nothing much of their background, their past history, their deepest beliefs, their fears. Hearing their dreams is like opening a novel at random and reading a single passage. You can understand what's being described to you only on the surface of it, the most basic description of what the character is doing and with or to whom, completely out of context. You get a sense of narrative style, of point of view, of tone, of diction and word choice and perhaps even the type of imagery invoked—all of which give you clues about what the characters and their author are up to. But *why* is any of this happening? you wonder. What does it mean?

Another of my former students also has recurring dreams about babies. She has a name for her dreams, too: she calls them the "articulate babies dreams." The "articulate babies" are never her own; she has only been given responsibility for them, and often they are in danger, too—and as tiny as they are, they can "speak like adults." They offer her "seemingly wise, but enigmatic, advice."

Out of the mouths of babes was what I thought, but I didn't say this. The phrase had not crossed her mind, as far as I knew, and besides, I had no idea what the phrase would have represented to her, why the babies in her dreams were able to give her good advice she couldn't understand. It isn't that the symbol "baby" or the idea of precocity—or advice that one somehow knows is the right advice if only one could make heads or tails of it—is by its nature opaque: it's only that the intersection between the symbols "chosen" from her stock of symbols and what those symbols meant to her was unknown to me.

Another student wrote to me about dreams in which she had "incredible upper arm strength." In dream after dream, she said, she'd "be walking through a doorway, or under a loft"—anything above her with a ledge that she could take hold of—and she would "grab on and start doing pull-ups."

I'm always amazed that I can do so many, so easily. I like how it makes me feel tough, as if proving to myself that I'm much stronger than I normally go about my life thinking I am. The pull-ups can happen anywhere, anytime— except of course in waking life, where I can't do a single one.

When she wakes up she is pleased and surprised (every time, surprised). I don't know what *arm strength* (especially as opposed to any other kind of strength) means to her, but I know it is meaningful that she exhibits it casually and constantly in dreams, and never in real life. If this were my recurring dream—if I were her—I'd think about this particular idea of strength that turns up again and again, at various times in her life—and not just that it's not a strength she actually has but that it's one she shows (or shows off) in the course of ordinary life in her dreams (she isn't Superman, after all, using extraordinary strength to perform heroic feats—or even a weightlifter, concentrating hard on the task at hand: she is merely passing by and pulling herself up). But it's not my dream, it's not my symbolic imagery, and while I admire the work of her unconscious in composing it, it doesn't tell *me* anything. Can recurring dreams of casual, easy, utterly surprising, passing-by-and-pulling-up strength—or endangered and/or dangerous babies—or wise babies—tell my former students something about who they are: how there are threads, or through-lines, that run through their lives? I am sure they can. And I am sure that their having told me these dreams with such urgency and precision suggests that they know it, too—even if they haven't determined what those threads may be. Even if they don't want to find out.

I always want to find out; I always believe I can, too.

These are twin convictions I never thought to question until I began to write about (or, probably more to the point, to read about) dreams and dream research. For I cannot imagine *not* seeing my dreams as portals—ways *in* that offer unparalleled access to places I wouldn't even know existed otherwise. How, I keep wondering, could anyone *not* take his dreams seriously?

Perhaps it's simply a matter of faith. The argument against the notion that our dreams provide useful information rather than a mishmash of cognitive trash, after all, is that we have no evidence they *do* (while we do have evidence of the brain chemistry, for example, that allows us—or forces us—to dream). Perhaps one accepts the workings of an unconscious mind or one does not—the way one believes in God or does not (and the sort of "evidence" that people of religious faith point to—of God's hand in everything around us—is, I suppose, not much different from the kind of evidence I rely on to support my own certainty: *surely you don't think any of this would be possible without . . . ?*).

The early anthropologist Edward Tylor's theory was that God itself (or multiple gods themselves) represented a primitive effort to explain phenomena such as dreams. (Later theories of religion, such as Mircea Eliade's, emphasized the longing for perfection, the quest for meaning, and the search for patterns; others—including Freud's—focused on why people were susceptible to beliefs that were irrational. Freud's emphasis, unsurprisingly, was on religion as an illusion, an unconscious neurotic response to repression.)

When it comes to religion, I've long suspected that if a child is not exposed to it early on, it's unlikely to take hold later—and by "exposed to," I mean something more than glancing or casual exposure; I mean directly and purposefully inculcated with, early and often (for certainly *I* was "exposed" to religious belief, through my grandparents, who I knew believed in God and whom I observed abiding by numerous rules they explained matter-of-factly: a Jewish person doesn't mix up *fleishig* and *milchig*, meat and dairy, or even the silverware she uses when she eats them; a Jewish person doesn't work on Saturdays—no, *mamaleh*, not even to make drawings or use the scissors. I even watched my grandfather pray every morning of my early childhood, wrapping himself in *tallis* and *tfillin*, and murmuring in Hebrew in the kitchen). I know, of course, that many people are inculcated with—bombarded by—the principles of their parents' religion in childhood and still reject it later, and also that there are people who seem to be temperamentally predisposed toward religion, so that it takes relatively little, by way of introduction to the idea of God, for their own faith to bloom. But it seems to me these are the exceptions to the rule, that faith is something we are taught to have when we are too young to consider what it would mean not to have it.

My grandparents were great influences on me in more ways than I can easily count, but the introduction to religion they provided, by their example, bounced lightly off me. Much more influential were the novels I read (a great many, very early—and certain of them, way too early—on) and my young mother's depression throughout my childhood, which led her to psychotherapy, the principles of which were casually but constantly introduced into my understanding of the way human beings worked (mostly by my father, who followed my mother into psychoanalysis and enthusiastically embraced its tenets).

There are those who argue that we humans are "hard-wired" to believe in God; I'm more inclined to think we're hard-wired to believe in *something*.

What I believe about dreams is this:

That our minds, "self-activated"—shut off to the world, turned on to themselves, by the not-very-quiet-after-all state we call sleep—have nothing *to* process but their own internal workings. In other words, once waking activity stops, once our minds cease to process what we're doing and what is being done *to* us—the sounds and sights and smells and tastes and feel of the "real world" (which is to say: experience, itself)—we are free to tune *in*, and what rumbles, troubling us, beneath the surface, takes over. And so we dream, simultaneously compressing into a manageable narrative package (however fractured or mysterious that narrative) those worries *and* expanding upon them, making narrative leaps, stringing together images and making metaphors, which themselves run the gamut from the obvious (missing the boat) through the collective (nakedness in public, the test for which one hasn't studied, extra rooms, flight—those metaphors we might as well think of as dream archetypes, they are made use of by so many of us), all the way up to the most intricate, complex, and wildly mixed (in the manner forbidden by English teachers everywhere).

For that matter, what rumbles *merrily* beneath the surface may be released too. It's true (Hobson, Hall, and Van de Castle have the numbers to prove it) that this occurs less frequently—and as I myself have noted, we are far less inclined to suppress what pleases us while we are awake, so naturally it isn't joy that's most often freed by sleep—but as someone who has (who has, and *remembers*) "good" dreams as well as bad, I can attest to the mind's peculiar way of burying the good news along with the bad. I have woken up happy, and full of wonder at my own happiness—and soon recognized that a dream had opened up for me the possibility of happiness, against which I had been holding a door shut tight (not daring to be proud of myself, or fully relieved, or even simply glad). If our dreams are little packages of worries that we are free (free at last) to turn our attention to once we are asleep, it is as if some dreams are tightly wrapped packages of "good" worries (worries about our own happiness? anxiety because there is something we are afraid to be happy about, or don't believe we deserve to be happy about? something our waking selves don't know we *can* be happy about?).

For those of us for whom analysis is instinctive, second nature— the default rather than a strategy—who have to be reminded (as Freud himself never said, but which is always attributed to him) that sometimes a cigar *is* just a cigar, dreams are the mother lode. Like poems, they can be examined for layers of possible meaning; like music, they introduce and set aside and reintroduce—in another key, in a slightly changed form—themes and counterthemes. Looking at a dream is like looking at a painting for a long time—see this! now this! and over here, look at *this!* A patch of color set beside another changes how you see them both. And the longer you look—or listen, or read—the more there appears to be before you.

And yet it seems to me nearly impossible for the undreaming mind to make symbols that accomplish as much at once as our dreams do. In our dreams, everything comes at once, jumbled together, knit together, complicatedly *arranged* together.

When my daughter and I, or my best friend and I, tell our dreams to each other, there will often be a moment, right in the middle of the description of a dream that's particularly convoluted and mysterious, when it will become suddenly obvious to the one telling the dream exactly how it fits into her understanding of her life—and that's part of the pleasure, part of the *use*, of telling our dreams: that sudden understanding, something unknown coming into the light.

It's the telling itself that allows this, I'm convinced. Just thinking over a dream doesn't work nearly as well—not for me, anyway, not for someone who relies on words, who has to turn everything *into* words in order to make sense of it—and that moment, that brightening, that abrupt clarity, when something hidden is revealed as surely and swiftly as if a curtain had parted to expose it, is the sort of moment I live for.

And a *shared* moment of understanding—when something complicated and mysterious suddenly makes sense to me that also makes sense to someone else, someone I love—this, for me, is nirvana.

There are many people, I think—my husband among them—who would consider this a confession, even a shameful one. Not because they are opposed to insight (my husband isn't) or even because they are opposed to taking dreams seriously (as far as I know, he still is). Glen, I think, would be appalled that understanding—especially the understanding of the secret workings of the unconscious, especially that sense of connection, of two secret selves making sense of each other—should be what I consider the heart of my experience of the world. He would argue that there are other, bigger things to focus on. Less *personal* things. As of course there are. But not for me.

Another dream about my grandmother:

She is living in the guest room of the little house I rented in Columbus before I bought the house I've lived in since, the one I'd hoped she'd live in with me. In the dream, the guest room is *in* the house I live in now. *The house I've been living in all along* is the phrase that describes it in the dream. She is lying in a full-sized, wonderfully comfortable bed (the very bed I had, in real life, on the night I had the dream, just bought for my daughter, to replace her old one), and she *is* comfortable, not in pain, but it is also clear that she is bedridden, and very old, as old as she was at the end of her real life. I'm aware that I'm going to lose her soon, and I'm worrying and fussing: I repeatedly go into the room to check on her, to ask if there's anything I can do for her (in the dream, I am not only fretful but disturbed by how strange it is that she can lie in bed *all* the time, not even having to eat or go to the bathroom: is there a tube, or several tubes, I can't see and somehow don't know about?), and she says no, no, I'm fine, I'm very comfortable. She sounds sleepy but not unhappy. This bed is wonderful! she says. It's so soft! Thank you! And I know I shouldn't worry. She's fine, I can see that. She's *with* me. But not for long.

In life, my grandmother was never above pointing out the obvious to me—she had no patience for subtlety (*that boy is no good; you shouldn't be with him*)—and in my dreams she seems often to return to point out what I already know but haven't spelled out for myself, and about which I cannot yet do anything (just as I couldn't bring myself to break up with the no-good boyfriend—a whole series of them, in fact). That is, I know what's making me unhappy but I can't fix it, so I am going to have to live with it for a while longer. But Grandma (dream-Grandma, just like the real thing) wants to make *sure* that I know, and that I don't forget.

The summer I had that dream, Grace was thirteen, and right down to the invisible lifelines I had nothing to do with (friends, theater, singing, manga and anime, *Twilight* and other novels *I* hadn't given her or recommended) and my reckoning with her not needing anything much from me at that point—or nothing, anyway, beyond what I had already given her, and continued to provide as a matter of course—my grandmother in the bed (*she's all right; you've done all you could; and she's still here—but not for long*) neatly spelled out the terms of my unease.

A year later, I would dream about living with Glen and Grace in an enormous apartment in Greenwich Village—an apartment so large that it had rooms I'd never used, rooms that I had never taken time to take stock of, though I had long been aware that they existed. All the rooms were full of someone else's belongings, and the three of us lived companionably among them.

In real life, we did something like this in the mid-1990s, when we lived for a year in Brooklyn Heights, in an apartment that belonged to a schizophrenic woman. She was living in a group home upstate, and Glen was renovating the apartment—we bartered his labor for rent—at the request of the woman's daughter and with the blessings of the mother, Pat. And in the course of my dream, the summer Grace was fourteen, I discovered that the Village apartment we were living in *also* belonged to Pat. The coincidence seemed remarkable even in the dream.

One day, in dreamtime, Glen and Grace were both out, and I decided to tour the apartment and determine what we might do with all the extra space. *Shouldn't we be using more of these rooms?* I asked myself.

Two things happened as I took my tour: I discovered that all of the rooms I hadn't made use of were crawling with small creatures — miniature chickens, frogs of all colors, mice, rats, scrawny little cats chasing the rodents and failing to catch them—*and* I got lost. I wandered so far, wringing my hands, jumping out of the way of the creatures (which frightened me), and looking in amazement at all the clothes Pat had left behind—racks hung with coats and jackets, sometimes multiples of the same one in different sizes, as if the room were a store—and wondering what we'd been thinking, choosing the particular set of rooms we had. Look at this big, comfortable-looking bed! Look at this dresser, its drawers full of shawls and belts!

Lost, I wandered out a door beyond a bedroom and down a set of cement stairs and ended up on a busy street, and within a few steps I couldn't even figure out how to return to *that* door. The entrance I knew, the one I'd been using for months—where was that one? I didn't even know the address of our building, I realized. I couldn't even remember what street it was on! I walked and walked, and I couldn't find it. I didn't know what would happen when my husband and daughter got home. I was afraid I'd never find *them* again.

The summer I had that dream was the worst summer I'd had in years—the worst summer I'd had in *decades*. Grace was going to start high school that fall, which filled me with a kind of anxious dread of which I had no prior experience, and which I did not understand. Did I imagine she was going to suddenly become the type of teenager I had been? Throw herself headlong into the sort of trouble I had seemed constitutionally unable to avoid? Turn her back on me the way I turned on *my* parents and even my grandmother?

But I wasn't only consumed with anxiety about Grace. I also seemed to have lost all confidence in my writing, in myself as a writer. For months, I'd been unable to write anything at all. I had no idea whether the two were linked, but I watched myself falling into so deep a depression I began to fear that the biological legacy of my mother's depression had at last revealed itself. I had always been confident that whatever genetic predisposition I might have had in this direction was adequately met—and countered—by an arsenal of coping and management tools with which my mother had never been equipped. Had I been wrong about this? I wondered.

I woke from my dream of the apartment full of someone else's things (the "someone else" a woman with a severe mental illness of a type that is generally accepted as both inheritable and stress-triggered), a dream of a spacious and well-appointed (if only borrowed) place I'd left and couldn't figure out how to return to, a dream of being lost and alone and afraid, and I was in tears. I woke up thinking, *Why did I think it was mine? It was never mine! What was I thinking, imagining I was living there so comfortably? How did I forget that it was only temporary?*

And: *Now I'll never find my way back to where I was. I'll never find the place where I'm supposed to be—a place I haven't been making full use of, anyway, and which I've allowed to fall into such neglect it's being colonized by pests.*

I'm going to lose everything I thought I had.

1

think sometimes that the real reason we want to tell our dreams is because they *are* art—the art that everybody makes. When we dream, said Nietzsche in *The Birth of Tragedy from the Spirit of Music*, we are each the "consummate artist." Dreams provide the universal opportunity to express oneself in metaphor. But the dreamer, as the psychoanalyst and writer Adam Phillips says (as Nietzsche himself must have known), is a most unusual sort of artist—"at once exemplary and anomalous"—for his only audience is himself.

And yet: *Look*, we say, and *listen*—isn't it amazing? Isn't it surprising?

Even when we don't know what our dreams are telling us, we want to relay them, we want others to behold them.

We want to be *seen*—just as our dreams want us to see them. We are not only our dream's only audience; we have—as Phillips reminds us in an essay called "Making Ends Meet"—"no choice in the matter." We cannot walk out; we cannot walk away.

Pay attention, the dream says. *I am telling you something about yourself.*

And we say: *Listen to my dream. I am telling you something about myself.*

Like all artists, dreamers not only have a stock of metaphors (Jung's *signs*) which they reach for again and again (I say *reach for* and not *fall back on*, because although we have them stockpiled, it *is* a reach, time and again, because they are not at hand but are tucked away, kept out of sight), but a set of themes, too. We all have ideas and feelings about our lives, about who and what we are, about *how life is*, that run so deeply and so broadly through us that we dip back into them repeatedly, whether or not they make sense in a given situation.

A woman I know, a novelist, often dreams about her ex-husband, although she hasn't seen him in many years, has no idea what has become of him, and never thinks about him, she says, when she is awake. In the dreams about her ex, she is trapped in either a small room or a small house—either way, the structure is "dingy and in disrepair." The dreams come unexpectedly and always let her know, she says, that she's in a bad situation (like her first marriage) that has her trapped. What interests me about her account of these dreams is that she *did* get out of her marriage, long ago, and never (consciously) looks back—so built into this unpleasant dream is something that doesn't appear in the dream itself, but must either be somewhere hidden in her understanding of the dream narrative as it recurrently turns up (that there *is* in fact an escape) or that doesn't figure in to her sense of how her own life has unfolded (that in fact she never really escaped—it only seemed as if she did) and who she is.

When she reported the small rundown place/ex-husband dream to me, along with her assessment of it, I didn't tell her what was on my mind. It's not always easy to stay quiet when you have an idea about somebody else's dreams, but it's my general rule—not only because it's none of my business (or because I'm as likely to be wrong as right) but because I don't believe that anyone *wants* to hear what I think their dreams might "really" be about—or that the same theme seems to run through many different dreams they've told me—or anything else, for that matter, about their private mysteries. Part of the urge to tell a dream must be to proclaim one's own mysteriousness, one's fathomless complexity. Even when the teller offers a succinct interpretation of her own, it doesn't really summarize the dream, doesn't fully reduce it to something easily explicable (otherwise, why not skip the recitation of the dream and go right to its undreamlike— earthbound—summary?). It marks it off, though: it's a way of saying *it's mine; here's the way I'd like it presented, the way I want you to think about it.* And so I don't offer up associations or ideas or analysis—I don't even ask questions—unless I am invited to. (And in all my life, only three people have ever issued such an invitation: my mother, my daughter, and my longtime best friend.)

Adam Phillips proposes that one of the reasons dreams are valued so highly (by those who value them at all—for, says Phillips in his essay "The Dream Horizon," when dreams are taken seriously they are always taken *very* seriously) is that there is a connection between obscurity and value, that cultures in which obscurity is associated with worthiness are those likely to prize dreaming. The paradox for the "dream valuers," Phillips says, is that it is when we are dreaming that we are both "most obscurely and most essentially ourselves."

Dreams *are* mysterious; they are—*we* are, each of us—unfathomably complex. Even the way dream images and scenarios recur from one dreamer to the next is tinged with mystery, something like the way we all choose from among the same words to make new sentences, new stories and poems, or the way the same twelve notes are recombined endlessly to make new music. We human beings personalize *everything*; dream symbolism is singular even as it is "collective." When finally I read the responses to my open call for dreams, I was astonished by the number of women who reported dreaming of babies in so many different ways: their own babies, when in real life they don't have children; the babies who have been entrusted to them; the babies in danger; the strangely articulate babies; the babies with magical powers. There were baby animals that needed to be nursed—and a dreamer who nursed them, always (she has been nursing the hungry baby animals in her dreams for over thirty years, she said); there are my starving, neglected baby animals; there are brilliantly, unusually colored baby animals, "walking around as if they were full grown though I know they're not," one woman told me. Babies may be a dream archetype, but no two dream babies were alike.

Nor two celebrities, even when they were the same celebrity. Numerous otherwise sober-minded academics, artists, and scholars who don't watch television or read *People* magazine reported regularly dreaming about pop culture figures—each making use of his own personal pop icon in his own way. I heard from those who relentlessly dreamed about their in-laws, or about neighbors they hadn't seen since childhood, or about packing a suitcase ("I have been packing that same suitcase for the last fifteen years").

My best friend—the one person to whom I am not related who is interested in hearing what I think about her dreams—had a recurring dream that plagued her, she said, for over thirty years, but that suddenly stopped "about fourteen years ago."

I'm in the backseat of the parked family car, motor running, with my little brother—one parent or other or both in the grocery store—and the car begins to back up and take off on its own. I'm too young to drive, can't see over the dashboard, etc.

The dream sounded to me like a turbocharged (or poeticized—not so surprising, not only because it's a dream, but because the dreamer is, as I have mentioned, a poet) version of her actual childhood: she'd been a child who'd felt, always, that too much was being left to her, who had to be grown up even when she was very young. But there was something else that struck me: the fourteen years since she'd last had the dream. Just over fourteen years ago was when she ended her first marriage and embarked on her second—a relationship that was exactly the sort of relationship she'd been longing for her whole life, which is to say a wholly encompassing one, in which her constant presence is required, literally and figuratively. This was something we had often talked about—the way, in this relationship, she felt necessary and desired—as well as another striking difference between her first and second marriages, which was that in this one she was able to relinquish control, surrendering to someone else's will and decision-making. When she told me about the dream, and when it had stopped, I thought about saying, "Right—fourteen years: you mean when you got together with _____?" but I also thought that if *she* had made that connection, she wouldn't have said "fourteen years"; she would have said "since _____." She didn't ask me why *I* thought she'd stopped having the dream, either; she'd even said "about" fourteen years, as if the timing weren't worth noting. And so I asked, cautiously, half-breaking my own rule, telling myself that I was not interpreting anything, merely asking a question, *and* that she would want me to ask: had she noticed that the two coincided? She had not.

And while this surprised me—she is not someone who fails to notice anything—I was even more surprised when, months after she had told me about the recurring dream she used to have (and leaving aside the curiosity that although we have traded many dreams over the two decades of our friendship, she'd never mentioned this dream before), she spoke of a childhood memory, one that still frightened her and which she'd also never talked about before. It was a memory of sitting in the backseat of the family car, her little brother beside her, the motor running, waiting for her parents to run an errand. "And they did this all the time," she said. "Why would they have? Why would they have left the motor running with two little kids in the car? What could they have been thinking?"

Why couldn't they have taken the kids with them, into the store or the bank or the post office? we both wondered aloud. Would that have been so much trouble?

"Maybe they couldn't find a legal parking place," I said doubt-fully, "and maybe it was cold out, so they couldn't leave you in the car without the heater on, and since there was nowhere to park, they *couldn't* take you out of the car. And maybe"—here I was on shakier ground—"it only happened once, on one very cold winter day, and it was so frightening you generalized the memory?"

And then later dreamed about it for three decades, I didn't say—because she didn't mention it. Because she seemed not to be thinking about her dream—her former dream—at all.

But I'm still thinking about it, although we haven't talked about it since—about the way she lifted a powerful image right out of her life, and made use of it so often for so many years. As a child she'd been terrified, she told me, that the car was going to start moving on its own, and she wouldn't know what to do. The memory—of the experience, of the feeling of the experience, whether it had occurred once or many times—had lodged itself in her, had become a sort of living metaphor.

And even after the metaphor ceased being "useful" in her dream life—even after she discarded it (or at least put it away; for who knows if it's really gone for good?)—she retained the memory; the memory still had the power to frighten her and make her angry.

When she told me the story of being left in the car in "real" life—her memory's version of real life—I thought about a dream my daughter first had when she was two and a half. Its central image came right out of a picture book I'd read to her that night before she went to sleep, in which the protagonist turned into a fish and then the whole world turned into an ocean filled with fish. The dream so terrified her that she not only woke up screaming ("I'm in the ocean, Mama! Make it go away! It's so dark here!"), she became afraid of the dark, as she had not ever been before: after this dream—which recurred, she has told me, many times—we had to leave a light on at bedtime (and not just a nightlight, but a true light, bright enough so that she could see everything in the room if she awakened) for years, long after most children are able to go to sleep in a dark room. And even now, although she is not afraid of the dark, and no longer dreams of the world as an ocean, she remains afraid of—and not just "afraid of" but deeply phobic about—life underwater: she cannot visit the aquarium; when people talk about scuba diving, or even snorkeling in shallow water on vacation, she shudders and turns pale. She cannot even bear to look at *photographs* of sea creatures.

The right metaphor at the right time worms its way into our minds—into our selves—forever.

It doesn't have to come in childhood, either. The hoard of dream-signs isn't finite, the way it was once thought that brain cells and mammalian ova were. Just as (we now know) females are *not* born with all the oocytes they'll ever need, and the brain's hippocampus keeps producing new brain cells, the storehouse of dream material doesn't shut down; it seems, in fact, to be infinitely replenishable.

I didn't learn to drive until I was thirty, and almost at once images of driving entered my dream repertoire—where they have remained, faithfully, long after driving has ceased to fill me with anxiety in my waking life. For years, though, I was sure I never would get used to it, I would always be tense and fretful behind the wheel. It's possible that it's not only the potent memory of how anxious I was when I first learned to drive—and how unwillingly I did so, pushed into it by a combination of geography (*You live in the Midwest now*, everybody said. *How can you* not *know how to drive?*) and a forceful boyfriend, who insisted on teaching me—but also the progression I've made, from fear and loathing to jittery acceptance to grim resignation to reasonably good-humored matter-of-factness (here, I tell myself, is something I know I never will enjoy the way many people claim to, but with which I have finally "come to terms"), that makes it a nearly perfect metaphor for me to reach for, one that's handy in all sorts of situations—a personal Swiss Army knife of dream symbolism.

In my driving dreams, I stop for a moment and the car abruptly vanishes, or I am obliged to drive a bus instead of a car, or I am a passenger *on* a bus and no one is driving it, although it's moving very fast (once, when Grace was six months old, I dreamed that I was on a bus racing along on a sheet of glass and I couldn't tell *who* was driving; there was an eighth of an inch of glass on either side of the bus and then a drop into the ocean—Grace's future nightmare imagery—heart-stoppingly frightening and yet beautiful, and I woke up in tears, breathing hard, and thinking, "but it was worth it"), or else I dream I am behind the wheel of my own car and I am lost, there are cars all around me and I can't see where I am supposed to be going. And then there was the dream in which I was hurrying—running late, as usual (or as had become usual; in my old life—in my life before I became a mother—I was always early), and, "as usual," I noted in my dream, there was nowhere to park. (In my waking life, for years, every place I dropped my daughter off and picked her up, including her school, was in an inconvenient location on a busy street on which there was no parking.) As I had done too often in real life, in the dream I left the car in a no-parking zone—I put the hazard blinkers on, a promise that I'd be back right away—and ran across four lanes of traffic. But just as I got to the entrance of the building, I glanced back, nervously—and saw that a tow truck was pulling away with my car, and that Grace was *in* the car.

"Where are they taking her?" I shouted to the people all around me, but they were all either too busy or too horrified by my naked terror to answer—even to say that they were sorry but they didn't know.

It wasn't until hours after I woke up that I remembered this: in the dream, Grace hadn't been upset at all to be towed away. She hadn't been happy about it, but she hadn't been afraid, either. She was nonchalant, I could see from where I was standing. *No big deal. Why are you making such a fuss, Mama?*

In real life, naturally, she would have been distraught (who wouldn't be?). But in my dream the point seemed to be that she *was* calm—cool, collected, sane, reasonable—even as I panicked and shouted and cursed myself, knowing "it was all" my own fault.

I often have such dreams: *it's all your own fault.*

And it occurs to me that in my dream my daughter was experiencing what my best friend feared so greatly both in her childhood and in her recurring dream of three decades, that the dream itself was a sort of reversal of my friend's dream: the parents in her dream are never seen, but they are to blame, implicitly, for the awful things that *might* happen at any moment; in my dream, I know I am to blame—I have done everything wrong—but even so, my daughter is all right.

Grace had her underwater dream at a time when everything seemed to be all right, but it wasn't. For one thing, she was at precisely the age when she was supposed to begin to "separate" from me—the point at which I was supposed to allow her to, or even urge her to, begin to grow up—but that wasn't happening: we were still as tightly bound together as we'd been when she was a baby. For another, her best friend that year was Silas, my old friend Vicki's son—we were living in Brooklyn then, temporarily, in the apartment that belonged to Pat, right next door to Vicki and her family, while I was on sabbatical from my teaching job—and although none of us would know this until after we'd moved back into our house in Ohio, Vicki already had cancer, was already on her way to gone.

That doesn't mean I think that Grace's dream was a message from the future. It just means that in retrospect it seems even more ominous than it did then—and also that her needing to have a light on all night long in the years that followed was only partly about her having had that dream. It was only the part that she could *see*.

. . . .

8

The ancient cultures were right: our dreams *are* a way of freeing us from our corporeal prisons so that we can wander for a while. We wander, every night, within ourselves.

Even the most apparently banal dream-journeys, the ones we all take—hastening down a school's long hallway to find the right room (*where is it? where* is *it?*), late for a test in a hard subject we know nothing of, the final for a class we didn't even know that we were taking—leave us feeling as if we've gone a long way.

It doesn't matter to us that we know that others have gone there before. Or, rather—knowing this does not make the journey any less *felt*, does not make it seem to have been less urgently taken. But it *matters*, all right, in the sense that such dreams let us know that we are more like one another than we can believe when we're awake, when our troubles seem so personal—when we cannot imagine that there's anyone who'd understand what it feels like to be us.

Adam Phillips speaks of dream-telling as a species of travel writing. *Here's where I went; here's what I did.*

I was not much older than Grace was when she had the underwater dream for the first time—when her best friend was a little boy exactly her own age whose mother would call me soon after we had returned to Ohio to tell me that "they" had found something, that she was scheduled for exploratory surgery—on the summer day that I lost sight of my mother and grandmother at the beach. I remember it perfectly—the noise, the crowds I couldn't see past, the feeling of the hot sand under my feet as I walked and walked—although it happened at least fifty years ago, and just that once, as far as I can tell. My mother and grandmother had been *right there* with the thermos of grape juice mixed with lemonade and tuna salad sandwiches wrapped in wax paper—and then they weren't. I wandered, searching for them, for what seemed like hours. I don't remember how I found them (with the help of a lifeguard? a policeman?), and my mother doesn't remember that I ever *got* lost at the beach, so I don't know how the story ends, except that I did find them, eventually, or they found me, and to this day I am afraid of crowds. To this day I dream of being lost in a crowd, pushing through people I can't see past, trying to find someone, becoming increasingly desperate. To this day, in my waking life, I have to make a great effort to overcome my fear of crowds—about which I am nearly as phobic as my daughter is about the deep sea and all the creatures in it.

y grandparents come and go.

    Cars are driven, towed away, lost. *I* am lost. There are crowds to be pushed through, animals in cages, broken telephones. There are all those rooms I didn't know I had.

And there are disasters.

Whenever I am feeling *very* bad in my waking life, my dream life turns to disasters.

My house has been bombed; the roof is about to cave in. Or a power line has been cut (but in the dream the power "line" is an obelisk—it looks like the Washington monument—and when it's "cut," it breaks cleanly in half: poisonous gas escapes from its center) and now there is no electricity—none anywhere in the world, because it was a "central line" that had been cut—and soon it won't matter, because the escaping gas is going to kill us all anyway.

Or: the sky darkens, turns a fearsome purple-gray. There is a terrible stillness, like when a tornado is approaching—one of my real-life fears (another late addition to my stock of dream imagery, thanks to the two years I lived in Nebraska, and in particular to the day a tornado touched down in my Omaha neighborhood, and while I cowered in my basement, as I had been instructed to by the same Midwestern-born-and-reared boyfriend who taught me to drive, it took the roof off the house next door).

The wind stops roaring, the trees stop trembling (that's when you know it's serious; a minute later there may be trees *flying*); the air feels heavy. Something dangerous-smelling is spreading. It's moving quickly, replacing the oxygen in the air, and there's nowhere to go to avoid it. Soon, I know, it will cover all of earth. It's just a matter of time—a matter of minutes—before we'll all be dead.

Or: everything looks and smells all right, but word has been passed from person to person, all over the world (a giant game of telephone:

whisper in the next person's ear), and now it's my turn. *Pass it on. The world is coming to an end.*

Once, for weeks, I had end-of-the-world dreams night after night. It was an anxious time. I had decided to take Grace out of school—she had just begun eighth grade—and teach her at home for the rest of the year. I'd told myself I had no choice: she wasn't learning anything, she was bored to death in school all day, and she was getting slammed with hours of meaningless, repetitive, busywork to do *after* school each day, by teachers who bullied and mocked her for thinking she was "so smart." But now, all day long, I'd worry and work, work and worry—I'd be teaching my own classes, advising students, going to committee meetings, running the household in all the usual ways, trying to sneak in some writing time, *and* writing lesson plans for Grace, giving her assignments when I left in the morning and coming home to read what she had written and talk to her about it, and wondering, all day, every day, if I were doing enough, if I were doing the right thing, if I could really handle this, if *she* could really handle it, if it were fair to her to have done this at all—and then at night, when I needed the relief of sleep, I would dream of the world coming to an end.

Night after night, the power failed and everything went dark, gases leaked, poison spread. I'd dream of planes that couldn't take off, that were racing on the ground at the speed of flight, destroying everything in their path—and the worst part, the scariest part, scarier even than the houses, buildings, bridges, *people* being mown down, was that I understood that the reason the planes couldn't get off the ground was that something had happened to the atmosphere itself, that this was a sign that something had changed for good in a way that spelled the end of humanity.

And one night, during that bad time, I dreamed of sitting with Grace at home and knowing (not knowing how we knew, but knowing) that it was "all over," and then turning on the TV and seeing that it was true: everything was in chaos, and the announcer was trembling as he asked people to stay calm, even as behind him everyone was running, crying, smashing into one another. "Now I am about to tell you what has happened," he said, "but please send the children out of the room before I do. There's no need for them to know what's coming."

When I wake from a dream of disaster, I always head straight to the window and open the curtains to see if it's true—if everything is gone, if the world has come to an end. I can see that it hasn't, but seeing isn't *quite* believing until I am fully awake. Until then, I'm still shaken, still frightened, still bracing myself for death. Sometimes I'll return to the window; sometimes I'll go downstairs and open the front door and stand on the porch looking out. *See? See? This is what's real.*

Only when I've been in the waking world long enough to dispel the dread and terror that I'd felt in the dream (sometimes this takes twenty minutes, sometimes several hours; sometimes it's *days* after a dream like this before I feel completely myself again, at home in the "real" world) am I able to remind myself that this is what dreams *do*: they pump up the volume, as if you can't know just how bad you feel unless the bad is blasting so loud you want to cover your ears.

In real life I know that whatever is troubling me is not "the end of the world." Or so I tell myself. I tell myself all day long: *Come on—this is not so bad. Everything will be all right.*

My dreams remind me that I'm faking it.

Was the decision to homeschool Grace *that* hard? Did I think the consequences of it could be that bad? Was I so anxious, so crippled by self-doubt, so overwhelmed, that it felt like doomsday?

I suppose it was, yes—and I did. I *was* that anxious, etc. All day, awake, I might have been able to keep anxiety and dread at bay, but not at night.

If the sleep scientists are even a little bit right about why we dream, if our experiences of crisis and terror in our sleep are meant (even only partly meant) to keep us in shape for the ordinary difficulties we're likely to encounter—as if, in our dreams, we're running double-time and with weights strapped to our ankles, training for a marathon—then it stands to reason that our dreams substantiate our worst fears. Mountains *must* be made of molehills. Uncertainty is nothing less than a worldwide power failure. The very air we breathe is poisonous.

The summer before Grace went back to school, leaving behind the awful school she'd gone to for so many years *and* gladly saying goodbye to her lonely year of homeschooling, was the summer I couldn't write, the summer I fell into a deep depression I vaguely understood to be largely about Grace growing up, a return (as I came to think of it) to putting "all my eggs in one basket." I didn't dream—thank goodness I didn't dream—about eggs in baskets. But I did begin to have disaster dreams again.

I couldn't believe it. It had been only a few months since the last bout of them—the every-night of them—had stopped. We'd gotten through the year of homeschooling, and although Grace had complained of loneliness, and she'd felt like "a freak," she told me, with everyone else she knew "going to school like a normal person," she and I agreed that it had been a good year, overall—an imperfect solution to an otherwise unsolvable problem. She had learned a lot; she had not been bored. She and I together had fallen in love with John Adams, wept over the Civil War, spent whole evenings talking about the Constitution or arguing about why Catherine loved Heathcliff. An English major concentrating in Shakespeare had come to the house once a week to read aloud and talk about the plays with her, and I'd found her a science tutor—a brilliant college student who turned dull eighth grade "physical science" into real physics and chemistry—and a Spanish tutor, one of my MFA students, who had her keep a dream journal and memorize poetry and songs in Spanish. Now that was all done, and she was busy with voice lessons and theater and singing camp and a summer reading and writing assignment for the public alternative high school she was looking forward to going to in the fall. Now I could—so I told myself—turn my attention back to my own work full time, as I hadn't really been able to do since before she was born.

But I could not work. Each day I tried, and each day I failed. Each day I felt worse; by midsummer I could hardly bring myself to get out of bed in the morning. I had never been so anxious and exhausted and defeated in my life.

We'd come from one crisis and almost immediately I was in another. I dreaded waking up in the morning to face a new day, and I dreaded going to sleep at night, to see the world in flames again.

The world ends—in flames or with poison, with bombs or with jets, under a purple sky, in silence.

A door opens—on a roof, in a basement.

The animals are in their cages, dying.

The rooms are full of furniture and dirty dishes.

Crowds gather and part, and I am lost.

I'm lost again. I'll never find my way—*again.*

And then one night, I fall in love. This is a new sort of dream, a narrative I've never spun before. I wake up feeling swoony, dazed, off balance, just the way you feel—just the way I remember feeling—when you've first fallen in love, when everything gleams with possibility and promise, before the day-to-day sets in. Before the bloom is off the rose.

Even five hours later, after dog-walking and e-mail and the Sunday *New York Times* and breakfast and lunch and a conversation with Grace about what she might study in college—linguistics? Shakespeare? voice?—I haven't shaken off the feeing, and it's both pleasant and disorienting. It's been a long time since I last felt this way, since I last had the sensation of falling-off-a-cliff-and-glad-about-it.

And even in my dream, it has been "a long time"—but in the dream I am much younger than I really am (although the time is also *now*, and in the dream I am worried about what is to become of my husband). The young man with whom I have fallen in love (and he is a *very* young man, just as I am a young woman in the dream: we are the age, in fact, of my own college students) is new to me, someone I've just met. I cannot quite but I can *almost* see his face as I recall the dream upon waking. It's no face I've ever seen before.

The young man is delightful. He is sweet and smart and funny, charming, serious, kind, lighthearted. He is perfect for me—he is the one I have been looking for all my life (so I think dreamily, in my dream).

But at the dream's end, just before I've woken up, he announces suddenly that he isn't sure *he* is in love with me. "We get along fine, and it's been great," he tells me, "but I don't feel like it's . . . you know, *love*. It's something else, I think."

But here's what's strange: that I woke up so *happy*.

In real life, in the twenty years before I met my husband, I'd been broken up with many times—so many times, in so many different ways, I'd be ashamed to list them here—and I was always shaken by these breakups. And not just shaken. A few of them left me flattened by grief.

But in my dream it mattered less that my beloved loved me than that I was in love. I was not *content*—the distinction was crucial in the dream—but I was *happy*. I even knew my happiness was fleeting, and I didn't care.

Months later, I am thinking, still, about this dream—the not-quite seeable face, the wistful *it's been so long*. What it was like to fall in love after so many years of the day-to-day of married life and parenthood. The careful dream-delineation of happiness versus contentment. What seems impossible in life: to accept *fleeting*.

It was the rare good dream, the dream that helps one reassure oneself—the dream that reaches for the place in the unconscious that knows better than the waking self does, that knows the *good*. It's easy to forget how to be happy (easy to forget to *be* happy), just as it's easy to forget that dreaming doesn't *only* open up a window to the darkness, the worries, the fears we hide from ourselves in daylight.

If, as Hobson would have it, we are driven "mad" in our sleep—driven mad *by* sleep: driven from our waking state into one in which sense, ordinary concentration, "paying attention," and orienting ourselves to what is around us are inhibited—we may also be driven sane. Sane as temporarily as *in*sane.

Our dream lives know both sides.

Our dream lives, it would seem, know everything.

Seeing Things

1

We were in the kitchen, cooking together. It was early January, early evening. We were cooking and talking. Chopping, pouring, beating, scraping, setting pans in the oven and on top of the stove—a great commotion of cooking, with plenty of clatter and mess (which is the way we like it, even now—or the only way we know how to do it, and thus we've come to like it; who can tell?)—and all the while talking. The stereo was on, too, the volume way up because it's in the living room, so that anyone passing through the living room on the way upstairs to what was then our only bathroom had to make the trip with her hands over her ears.

Grace was seven and a half. We were doing a lot of cooking together that winter, that whole year. A lot of cooking, a lot of talking, a lot of listening to music. I don't remember what was on the stove that night—and in the oven and on the cutting board and in the mixing bowls—and I can't say *what* music we were listening to, turned up so loud, or what we were talking about. If I were writing fiction, as I used to only do, I would be able to tell you. Not being able to say—having to guess, because I don't want to pretend that my memory is better than it is—is part of why I never used to be interested in writing nonfiction. The other part—not unrelated—has to do with what I once thought of as being "constrained by" what actually happened: stuck with and tied down by—*weighed* down by—the inartfulness of "real" life.

But as I have grown older, I've found that what actually happens is in fact at least as interesting to me as what I can make up, and that real life, when looked at closely, is enough like art that the distinction between what *is* art and what isn't is less interesting to me than it used to be.

(*Art* may be the wrong word. *Artful* might be better. For that matter, *interesting* may be the wrong word. What I mean by *interesting*, I think, is *meaningful*. But let's let this be for now. I'll come back to it: it's one of the things I most want to talk about. But first things first. I have a story—a true story—to tell.)

My best guess is that on this night we were making the meal we ate most often in those days—pasta with a sauce heavy on the garlic, the tomatoes pureed in the Cuisinart; collard greens or broccoli sauteed in olive oil and still more garlic; and, for dessert, the cake we called "healthy pound cake," which Grace and I had invented together that autumn (and which we called "healthy" because it was made with whole wheat flour, no white at all, and never mind the three cups of sugar and half pound of butter)—and that the music was the Beatles (because 2001 ushered in the Era of the Beatles in our house).

We were almost certainly talking about school, because winter break had just ended, and it was that January that Grace made her first friend at the school she'd transferred to eleven months before. Chances are good that she was telling me about her—Kristin—because most nights, that winter and spring, Kristin was the main topic.

Or she might have been talking about her teacher, the tirelessly inventive Mrs. Pace, and some complicated project she had just assigned—for second grade was not only Year One of the Era of the Beatles, it was also the Year of Complicated Projects: a to-scale model of the Capitol Building, a homemade katydid costume Grace wore while reciting a poem she'd written about katydids (she got to choose the insect; I was just grateful she hadn't picked one that had more legs), a possum made out of pantyhose and pillow batting, an "original invention" related to the Olympics (for which Grace came up with something she called "Snack 'n Drink").

What I do remember perfectly is that right in the middle of everything—*in mitn derinnen*, as my grandmother would have said—Grace stopped what she was doing and said, "Mama?"

She said it quietly, but even with all the kitchen clatter and the music blasting I still heard her. She said it in an *arresting* way, the way that makes everything else go quiet, no matter how loud it had seemed a minute before. Then she said, "Don't freak out." She was looking around the room. "Something weird is happening."

She didn't sound frightened, only puzzled, so I tried—as I have always tried; as I still try, with variable success—to do as she asked.

Instead of freaking out, I kept on doing what *I* was doing, with knife and chopping board or wooden spoon and mixing bowl or pot or pan. I looked away, too—looked at the table, at the mess we'd made in the center of the kitchen—because I knew she'd be more likely to keep talking if I did. But even as I kept in motion, kept my eyes off her, I could feel my own alarm like a pinprick's worth of blood spreading, staining the fabric covering a wound.

"What is?" I asked her. I said it calmly. I had learned over the past year not to let her in on my alarm. You'd think I wouldn't have had to *learn* this; you'd think I would have known from the beginning that picking up on my distress would increase hers, or would make her distressed when she hadn't been. You'd think I would have known that, as close as we were, it would have been impossible for her *not* to pick up on my anxiety if I didn't consciously mask it. But there are lots of things it now seems to me I should have known and didn't—things I had to teach myself about being a good mother.

It's possible this is true for all parents. I honestly have no idea. To me, not knowing—having to work at it, and making mistakes—felt like failure, always.

"You're very, very small and far away," Grace said. We were standing catty-corner around the tile-topped table we used as a kitchen counter. We were no more than two feet apart. Now I looked up at her. Her eyes were wide and she was pale, but she still didn't sound frightened. "You're *tiny*, Mama. You're *way* at the other end of the room and the room is very long—like a long hallway. You're so small it's like you're a mile way."

"I'm right here," I said. I lifted my hand and held it up the way you do when you're swearing to tell the whole truth, nothing but the truth, so help you God. "Does my hand look far away? It's right here by you." I lowered it to touch her hand. Grace looked down at our two hands.

"It's small and far away. *My* hand is far away and small, too."

We stood there looking at our hands. Then she looked up. "Oh!" she said. "You're very near now. *Very* near. And big." Her voice was full of wonder, and suddenly she laughed. It occurred to me that I ought to try to make myself laugh, too—to mirror her. But I could not. What I felt was that my heart, always overfull when it comes to Grace, had been pierced.

"You're huge," she said. "Mama, your face is *huge*."

It was strange — stranger, I mean, even than it sounds, because right then I *felt* huge; I felt swollen. I held on to the table and felt my heart swelling into every part of me. I could even feel it beating in my fingers where they met the table's edge. And my fear, like blood, filling me everywhere.

For a minute we just stood there — Grace staring at me in amazement because I was so big; I, listening to my heart thump in my fingers, my legs, my feet, and feeling as if I were about to burst.

And then: "Oh — everything's normal again." She let out a long breath. "Wow. Wow. *That* was weird." She picked up her spoon and got back to work.

In the little slip of silence that followed, I studied her. Then, quietly, "casually," I asked her if she hadn't been scared. *I* was still scared. (Even now, thinking back, writing about it for the first time, I'm *still* scared.)

She hadn't been scared, it turned out, because this wasn't the first time it had happened. It had been happening, on and off, for a week or two. And this was the third time *today*. She told me this, and then without waiting for me to ask the question, she answered it: "I didn't *tell* you because I was afraid it would scare you."

"Right," I said. "Sure."

I was still sounding as if I were taking it all in stride, but I was heartbroken (that she'd been experiencing these hallucinations all week without telling me, that my seven-year-old had felt she had to keep something this unnerving to herself, for what she thought of as my sake), terrified (by the possibility — the first thing that had occurred to me — that something physical, something terrible, was wrong with her: a brain tumor, a stroke — or was she going blind?), and full of dread and worry, because the *second* thing that had occurred to me was that it wasn't physical, that it was entirely a product of her mind — truly a hallucination.

I asked her what had made her tell me now. And she said, "I thought I'd better." She whispered, "*You* know."

I did know. For Grace, the battle between wanting to tell me everything, and trying to draw a line between herself and me, to establish herself as a separate person with experiences and thoughts of her own to which she was entitled, had been a conscious and considerable one for nearly a year by then (and perhaps longer than that, but it had been *visible* for a year).

It may be that this battle is always considerable for a child, especially one who's particularly or unusually close to her mother, but I know it isn't always conscious. It hadn't been for Grace, either—or for me, helping her—until she was six and a half years old. And certainly the sorting and appraisal that she was still undertaking a year later (*this* needs to be told, *this* is all right to keep secret) isn't a full-time occupation for most children, but rather a process, a part of growing up. For Grace it wasn't so much a process as it had been a crisis.

The crisis had occurred almost exactly a year before this moment in the kitchen when things got smaller, then bigger. At six and a half, not long after she started first grade, Grace began to exhibit a constellation of bizarre symptoms. She began saving trash—at first, anything she'd touched (paper on which she'd made a single mark, price tags clipped from new clothes, the crumpled wrapping paper torn off gifts), then anything she'd *seen* (an empty juice box in the playground, a pencil stub on the floor in school, the discarded giftwrap from other children's presents). She started needing to make everything come out even—if she bumped one elbow, she had to bump the other—and to check and recheck her towers of stuffed animals. But what alarmed me most was that when I collected her from school she would launch into a panicked monologue in which she reported everything that had happened that day *and* everything she had thought or felt, along with whatever flew into her mind, no matter how trivial or fleeting, as she reported it. This would go on all afternoon and into the evening. At bedtime she would sob, because going to sleep meant she could not continue to tell me what was on her mind.

This went on for several months—months during which my six-and-a-half-year-old daughter was a walking, talking, trash-saving, tic-cing, compulsively checking, stream-of-consciousness narrative.

But nearly a year had passed; she was *fine* now. That was what I kept telling myself—trying to calm myself—that January night as we finished up our work in the kitchen and brought plates to the table in the dining room, turned off the stereo so we could talk over dinner, sat down to eat the meal we'd prepared together. She was fine; she'd *been* fine for a long time.

Fine, I thought—not *cured*. I never used the word *cured*. I didn't—

don't—believe in "cures" when it comes to psychological troubles. And psychological troubles, not a physiological disorder—not a bio-chemical imbalance, not a genetically programmed disease—had turned out to be what were at the root of Grace's symptoms the year before. What I learned from the excellent psychiatrist and psychoana-lyst Sarah Knox, who was willing to take the time to find out what was wrong with my daughter, I have written about at length in another book, so suffice it to say here that the great discovery we made—the psychiatrist, my daughter, and I—was that Grace and I had been too close for too long: so close that it was hard for my daughter to tell where I left off and she began. This (as Dr. Knox pointed out) is quite natural in the relationship between infants and their mothers; it was entirely unnatural in a six-year-old.

Grace's symptoms were vanquished when, guided by Dr. Knox and later by another psychoanalyst, a clinical psychologist named Janet Meltzer, we made a series of changes at home that were de-signed to let her begin to grow up, to find out for herself that she was indeed a separate person who could manage some things (even many things) without any help from me. In a year she had made extraordi-nary progress. But she wasn't *fine*.

I should have known better—that's what I told myself later.

I suspect that I did know better but couldn't bear to think about it.

Symptoms, as Adam Phillips says, *can* be cured—but there is no cure for the unconscious.

It took nearly a week before we could eliminate the most frighten-ing physical causes for what Grace had experienced on that January night when she told me how small, then big, I seemed. The first stop was the pediatrician, who found nothing unusual on examination and nothing in Grace's medical history—or in mine or my husband's or either of our families' (the emphasis was on migraines, of which none of us had any history)—that provided any clues. Next we saw the pediatric ophthalmologist who had performed eye muscle surgery on Grace when she was two, when her eyes had suddenly crossed. "She's doing great," he told us. "Her vision is excellent—perfect." When I asked him what he thought might be responsible for what had hap-pened, he said, "Oh, you know, kids can sometimes *make* that sort of thing happen just by staring at something long enough."

In the elevator, a few minutes later, Grace asked me if he had been suggesting that she was making things get smaller, then bigger, on purpose. "Why would I do that? Why would anyone?"

I told her I was sure he hadn't meant it that way. "He just meant it's nothing to worry about."

"*I* wasn't worried. You were."

True. I still was. And I didn't know what he'd meant, really, either. "I think he just doesn't know how to explain what happened. Doctors don't know everything, after all."

"Well, they should," she said. "Don't you think?"

Our last stop—"just to be safe, just to be sure," our pediatrician said—was for a CAT scan of Grace's brain. At Children's Hospital, she lay flat on her back with one of her favorite stuffed leopards, Liliana, tucked under her arm, and I had to step out of the room as girl and leopard ("just like a piece of carry-on luggage at the airport," Grace remarked later) were swallowed up and spit out, again and again, by the scanner.

Her eyes were fine; her brain was fine (and so was Liliana the leopard's). Now what? I wanted to know.

"Now nothing," our pediatrician, Eileen Sheets, said. She sounded cheerful. "Look, it's a mystery. Some things just *are*. What's important is for you to know there's nothing to worry about."

Dr. Sheets always sounds cheerful. She *is* cheerful, I think. And she is a genuinely kind person, too. She's amiable, she's warm, she's reassuring, and she's reassuringly *smart*. She is also both pragmatic and optimistic. I have always trusted her. I *like* her. And I was grateful—deeply grateful—as well as immensely relieved that there was nothing physically wrong with my daughter. But "some things just *are*" wasn't going to cut it. This might well be the end of the line for the physician, I thought, but for me it was just the beginning.

Years later, another physician, a friend, would use the word "idiopathic" to describe what happened to Grace that January night (and what would continue to happen from time to time over the years, until it stopped—as far as we can tell, for good—before she turned fourteen). "Idiopathic" meant, essentially, *some things just are*—but with a doctorly gloss, implying that the cause was still at least theoretically under consideration (or, at the *very* least, that it mattered)—even if it was, alas, presently "unknown or obscure." *Idiopathic* is a diagnosis that says, *Oh, hell, I give up—for now, anyway.*

Dr. Sheets was saying something that seemed braver and more

honest, something along the lines of, *I don't know—we* can't *know. We must accept that we can't know everything, because, let's face it, this is how life is. There will always be some unknowable things.*

Of course, that she was being honest—even brave—didn't mean that I agreed with her.

Adam Phillips, in his book *Terrors and Experts*, describes symptoms, from a psychoanalytic point of view, as secret ways of asking for something. At one time, my daughter had been full of secrets: her longing to be a separate person, and her terror of that longing; her desperation to take charge of herself, and her fear of being in charge; her wish to shake me loose and begin growing up, begin to be on her own—and her horror of growing up, being on her own, and losing me. These secrets revealed themselves through metaphors—for what are such symptoms but metaphors?—that she herself didn't understand. She wept every time she had to throw anything away; she was desperate to make everything come out even—a process she called "catching up"; and she talked nonstop, without taking a breath, without editing, without pause, without any ability to stop herself, even when she began to cry—she would talk and cry at the same time—terrified that if she didn't tell me what had passed through her mind it would mean that it had never passed *through* her mind.

Now, a year later, assured that she was physically healthy, I was ready to look at the rogue symptom (as I had begun to think of it) as a metaphor.

It is an article of faith that novelists and poets (or the writers of "literary essays" like this one) will turn to metaphor when they reach a point at which language, "ordinary" language, fails them—when ordinary words that will tell the reader what something *is* without invoking anything outside it won't do the job that needs to be done, or it would take so many words to do a job that metaphor can do quickly, more efficiently, much more precisely. As rich as language is (and for whom is it richer than for a writer?), there are times when it seems to us that we are attempting to describe something that will require more precision than "mere" words can capture (something too small for the naked eye to see). But words are all we have (not microscopes, not telescopes, not electrodes to connect one brain to another so we can *show* our readers exactly what we mean), and so we make use of words in a way that transcends their ordinary (even their most elegant, even their most beautiful but still "ordinary") use: we use them to sketch a picture of what *we* are seeing, feeling, thinking, experiencing. It is almost exactly *like this*, we say. You know what *this* is, yes? So now just imagine that *this* is *that*.

That is what a metaphor does on the page. In life—the unconscious is the artist making metaphor.

Symptoms are not only secret ways of asking for something but are ways of telling us—the world—exactly what it feels like to be oneself. And that too leads to a question: *Will you understand what it means to be me?*

This is, of course (I say "of course" but I realize that this is *not* an "article of faith," since my own students so often resist the assumption), what a novelist does when a character comes alive on the page. Let us say, then, that it is *my* article of faith. For a character to be real—to move the novel's readers to believe in him or her, to allow them to become "lost" in a book the way they hope to and to experience the world through that character's consciousness—we *must* understand what it means to *be* that character.

This is not so much a matter of our seeing what characters do, or what they encounter as they go about their lives, but being able to see what they do *with* their experiences: how they process the world as they encounter it. In my teaching, I talk about this as the protagonist's "experience of the experience"; I talk about the experience itself—whatever that may be: hearing bad news, running into an old friend on the street, walking through a busy airport, getting slapped across the face—as "raw material" for our characters. As a writer, what I'm interested in is the psychological, sensory, emotional, and intellectual space between the encountering of the "raw material" of life, and how each of us will take that in and make sense of it. What I want to capture is the moment (or the moments) *before* interpretation—before naming, classifying, and summarizing the experience for ourselves—occurs. It's in that processing, that taking in and making sense of, that we each differ so dramatically—so characteristically—from one another; it's there that a reader will have the chance to find out what it means to be the character doing this "processing."

The interpretation that follows it is interesting, too: what we each make of what we've just experienced, how we put it together with everything else we know. And what comes before the experience is interesting too — that is, what each of us *are* in some essential way, some pre-experiential way (what, let us say, we are genetically programmed to be). It is all of this, taken together — everything we were "born to be," everything we have experienced, how we experience each new thing we experience, and what we tell ourselves about it — that makes up what we think of as our "selves."

In life, it seems to me, we are forever trying to show others who we really are, even when we don't know that's what we are doing.

And the unconscious — it is busy, also, always trying to show *us* who we really are. Alone in our selves, we are both authors *and* readers.

From my point of view, if there were no physical reason for Grace to see things — to see me, in particular — as nearer, then farther, than reality would have it (and perhaps even if there were *also* a physical cause — if, for example, as both Dr. Sheets and my physician friend later suggested might happen, Grace someday developed migraines, and this phenomenon was seen as an early precursor to migraine syndrome), that didn't mean there was no *other* cause. I was not satisfied with either *I give up! I just can't figure it out* or *We're not meant to know everything*, and not just because I wanted to know what was going on, but because I believe that knowledge, that understanding, is always possible — that although the reason something happens may not be clear at first (or even second or third — or twenty-eighth, or two hundred and seventh) glance, no reason is so obscure that it can't be teased out eventually. With enough time, enough effort, enough *thought*.

I'd say that I would stake my life on that principle, but I already have. That is, I've staked my life — my work, my understanding of the world (and of my daughter; of myself) — on the very idea that everything has meaning. And that its meaning can be seen if only one looks closely enough.

When Grace was six and a half, I had had no idea what she was experiencing until she became symptomatic, and so it was those symptoms (the trash-saving, the "catching up," the panicked stream-of-consciousness monologues) that saved her: they revealed the secrets she was keeping—keeping even from herself—so that she could be helped. By the time she had her first experience of what we would come to call the "Getting-Smaller-and-Getting-Bigger," she and I had worked our way through the roughest part of what I had learned was a crisis of separation/individuation. I still had to make a conscious effort to treat her as a separate, and competent—if very young—person (who would let me know if she needed me for something); *she* had to work hard, too, to think of herself that way. As I've said, one of her struggles in the wake of the crisis of the year before was to fig-ure out the difference between things she *should* tell me—the things a parent needs to know—and what was meant to be her own, her pri-vate thoughts and feelings, or else was simply not necessary to report. When there were things she wanted to tell me that she knew weren't essential for me to know, she had to work out a complex answer to what should have been (what would have been to another child, reared differently) a simple question: *why* do I want to tell Mama this? Because it will be interesting to talk about, fun to tell, or she'll enjoy it—or because I feel as if, if I don't tell it to her, it isn't real to *me*?

Complicating this already complicated business was her hypersen-sitivity to my responses (indeed, her hypersensitivity to my responses was itself another symptom of the trouble between us). When she hurt herself—scraped her knee, twisted her ankle—or had a stom-ach ache or a sore throat, she would often hesitate to tell me because she found she couldn't tolerate my reaction. "No *sympathy*," she would say, not pleading but scolding (and sometimes shrieking, when she was seriously in pain—because then my sympathy didn't just upset but enraged her).

That was how I knew, when she told me about Getting-Smaller-and-Getting-Bigger, not to overreact. How I knew, in fact, not to re-act at all. And when she told me that it wasn't new, that she'd kept it from me all week, but that finally she felt she had to tell me, I knew how hard she had thought about this, and struggled with it. And I knew she was watching me for a reaction to this disclosure, too.

She had coached me all year about how I was supposed to deal with her reports of anything that could be categorized as painful or problematic—not just physical distress but a disappointment or hurt feelings or a mistake she realized she had made. I was to acknowledge what she'd told me, and if there were questions to be asked (*How* did you fall? When did your head start to hurt? What did you do when she said that?), I was to ask them, but as briskly and dispassionately as possible.

I believe I know why she so disliked my sympathy, too, even though she wasn't able to explain it. I think she had sympathy confused with empathy, and she didn't *want* my empathy—she didn't want me to feel what she was feeling. Indeed, by the time she was seven and a half, she had swung to another extreme: unable to abide my sharing any painful experience with her. And I suspect that even as my sympathy, which she experienced as empathy, felt intolerable to her, she must have craved it, too—and despised herself for craving it. My sympathy, then, for her—my sympathy and her response to my sympathy—was another metaphor; indeed, it might have been a metaphor for everything that was troubling about our relationship.

The only surprise to me now, thinking back on those first moments when Grace told me that I had become very small, then very big, is that I didn't interpret this new symptom—the rogue symptom—immediately. Interpretation, as I have already suggested, is an occupational hazard for me (though I admit I've often wondered which came first: the occupation or the inclination). Grace is pretty good at parsing metaphors, too (the occupational hazard, perhaps, of being a novelist's daughter). She learned all about them before she'd even started school, because we spent a lot of time together in those days (or, you might say, because I never let her out of my sight in those days)—long days, *pleasant* days, during which we talked a great deal even as we made collages or dioramas or as I drove to the playground or pushed her in a swing once we got there—and I explained a lot of things to her in the course of an ordinary day (mainly to keep myself from going crazy, but also because she actually seemed interested). About metaphor, when I first mentioned it, she said, "It sounds more like a dessert than something about words," but by the time she was five and watching *The Wizard of Oz* on video for the second time, she leapt up from the couch when Dorothy sang the line about the place "over the rainbow" where *troubles melt like lemon drops*. "Mama!" she cried. "Troubles don't really melt! That's a *metaphor*." And before I could respond—no doubt I was going to clap my hands—something else occurred to her. "Wait—*troubles*. That's the Wicked Witch. *She's* trouble. And *she* melts. Remember, Mama? She *melts* at the end!" So then I had to tell her about foreshadowing, too.

What strikes me as most curious, actually, is that the symptom/metaphor that appeared so suddenly, a year after the others had resolved, was such a heavy-handed one, one I'd be loath to use in fiction. You would think the unconscious would be more subtle—a better artist. But it seems clear to me that Grace at seven and a half was ready for me to *be* smaller and less significant, that she needed to put some distance between us—and also that I loomed large, still. And my guess is that she still wanted me to "loom large"—that just as much as she'd had it with my being such a big presence in her life, she still longed for our continuing closeness. Thus: Getting-Smaller-and-Getting-Bigger.

A classic conflict made—literally—visible.

3

It was a highly unusual symptom, I was told. It was so unusual that Janet Meltzer, the psychotherapist Grace had been seeing since "the problems"—as Grace always referred to what had happened the year before—had never encountered it, so unusual that there were no published studies of it as a psychogenic symptom at all (probably, Dr. Meltzer suggested, because the sample was so small). She put in a call to Sarah Knox, the psychiatrist who had initially seen and diagnosed Grace, in Cincinnati, during the earliest time of "the problems" (when I had made the four-hour-roundtrip drive from Columbus once or twice a week, after failing to find a psychiatrist in Columbus who was willing to do something more than match Grace's symptoms to the drugs known to treat them successfully). I hadn't talked to Dr. Knox since she had first delivered us into Dr. Meltzer's hands, but I knew that the two therapists had kept in touch about Grace.

Dr. Knox, as it happened, *had* heard of our rogue symptom, but only twice before. In her extensive practice dedicated to children and adolescents, she had encountered it in just two teenage girls—both unusually intelligent, and both with similar psychological profiles to Grace's, Dr. Meltzer reported, which was to say, girls with "separation/individuation issues around their mothers."

Well, there it is, I thought. It had been almost too easy to track down—all it had taken was a couple of phone calls. Mostly I was just relieved to hear that *someone* had come across the symptom in her practice. It gave me the vague idea that someone (and not just someone, but our own brilliant Dr. Knox, whose diagnosis and wise, straightforward, practical advice had cured Grace of every one of her earlier symptoms, by addressing what was at the root of them) was on the case. I wondered aloud, to Dr. Meltzer, if it were possible that other children, even if only other bright girls with "individuation issues," had experienced the phenomenon but simply not reported it. Dr. Meltzer conceded that it was.

And that was that.

I told Grace what I'd learned, and it satisfied her, too. And as time passed, and the Getting-Smaller-and-Getting-Bigger continued to visit her periodically, she became accustomed enough to it that she took it in stride when it came, and figured, as I did, that sooner or later she would outgrow (or "get over") it—just as sooner or later she supposed she would be able to spend the night at a friend's without panicking—just as she had stopped saving trash, stopped compulsively checking, stopped "catching up."

And really, that the symptom was almost unheard of, even by Dr. Knox, didn't surprise me very much. Leave it to *my* daughter's unconscious, I thought, to invent an almost entirely original (even if rather ham-fisted) metaphor.

And the story would perhaps have ended there—though it's not much of a story, is it? (And that's another reason, besides the limitations of memory, and the constraints of truth, that I avoided nonfiction for so many years. Life doesn't fall out into *story* very often, and what's required to shape it into story is suspiciously like writing fiction, but without the considerable pleasures of making things up. So it seemed to me. But that was before it occurred to me that I could ruminate—and not just tell *true stories*—and since I so often long to ruminate in fiction, and will not allow myself to do so nearly as often as I wish to, essay writing all at once became enormously appealing.)

The story *didn't* end there, as it turned out.

It didn't end there because of something that happened the summer Grace was eleven.

She and I were away from home together, at a three-day retreat for the Columbus Children's Choir, into which she'd just been accepted. The choir had set up the retreat in preparation for the singing year ahead, with full days of rehearsals and short breaks for games and swimming, and Grace—who had never gone to "sleep-away" camp before and was worried about whether she'd be able to handle it, but didn't want to miss the retreat and start her first year with the choir feeling out of step—had come up with a compromise solution to the problem it presented: *I* would go, too, as a volunteer counselor for a group other than hers, sleeping in a different cabin and spending my days looking after other people's children.

Columbus Children's Choir ("The Voice of the City") is actually nine separate choirs, and Grace, upon her audition, had been accepted as a "Santa Maria," the (musically) advanced middle-school-age group. I was to be a counselor for the "Pintas," a group of beginning singers ages eleven to thirteen. (And yes, there is also a group of "Ninas." For that matter, there is an "Isabella," and a "New World." But I digress.)

The first day of the retreat was all about learning to breathe properly, about posture and mouth-shaping and solfege (*do, re, mi*) and the Curwen-Glover hand signals for each tone of the scale (the choir uses a teaching method known as Kodály, which in turn is based largely on the work of John Curwen, a nineteenth-century English congregational minister whose emphasis was on aural perception and "audition"—or mental hearing—and regards sight-reading as the foundation for a musical education). I sat silently in a corner during the Pinta rehearsals, trying to memorize everything the children were learning, and except for a brief flutter of anxiety at bedtime (Grace came to my cabin to say goodnight, and wept, and went off to her own cabin as if sentenced to death; then I went into my cabin and cried), everything went well.

The next morning, Grace hailed me on the road to breakfast and fell into place with the girls from my cabin and me. After a while, girls fanning out here and there, it was just Grace, one remaining Pinta girl, and me, approaching the mess hall. Grace had already told me how much fun she'd wound up having the night before—everyone had stayed up late whispering and giggling, then they had all "passed out," they were so tired, and she hadn't even had time to worry or be frightened—and I'd said, "So you'll be fine tonight then," and she'd scowled at me: "I *doubt* it." Now she was telling us—the Pinta girl and me—about a game the girls in her cabin had played, sitting in a circle on the floor of the cabin, before they got into their sleeping bags, and then Grace dropped her voice and said, "But you know what else, Mama? It happened again—that thing."

I knew immediately what she was talking about, even though by then it hadn't happened—or she hadn't mentioned that it had happened—in several months, and what struck me first was that "it" had happened on a night when I was elsewhere. It was unusual, though not unheard of, for her to experience the Getting-Smaller-and-Getting-Bigger when I wasn't there, but this particular visitation seemed "logical" to me, given the circumstances: I was nearby, but out of sight; she was staying in a cabin with strangers—girls her own age as well as two counselors, parent volunteers, whom she'd never met before that day. This was for Grace a major undertaking, something truly out of the ordinary. But I didn't have a chance to ask her any questions; the girl on my other side said, "What happened? What *thing*?" and Grace, who never seemed to mind talking about this—or about "the problems" she had had when she was six—explained. The Pinta girl gasped and grabbed my arm. We all stopped walking. "No!" she said to Grace. "Are you kidding me? You're kidding me, right? That happens to you? You see things like that?"

This child had hardly said a word before then—not to me or the other Pinta counselor, and not to the other Pintas. Whenever I glanced at her, her face was very still, impassive. And yet she had responded to my attempts to engage her in conversation with a look of longing so acute—if fleeting—it made me want to hug her. I imagined that she was nervous about being away from home on her own, that perhaps she had been induced against her will to attend the retreat (or even to join the choir—since her impassivity had extended to her singing during the previous day's rehearsal), and that by nature she was shy, reserved, not a talker—a sort of person by whom I am always puzzled, never mind that I am married to one of them (but then, he puzzles me too). I watched her now as Grace said, noncommittally, "Sometimes, yeah. It's pretty weird, I know." I saw the girl's face change. "It's weird all right. I can't *believe* it." She said this passionately, in a rush. She seemed to have become another child altogether. "Really—I just can't believe it." Her fingernails were digging into my flesh just below the sleeve of my tee shirt. "This has been happening to me *all my life*. I mean, since I was *little*. And my brother—it happens to him too. But he's never told anybody, anybody but me, and *I've* never told anybody but him. I didn't even know it happened to him till, like, a couple of weeks ago. He just *told* me. Neither of us ever told anybody else because we figured they'd think we were crazy—they'd send us away."

"Wait," I said. "Send you where?"

But she was still talking. She was talking a mile a minute. She and her brother, she said, didn't live together; they had never lived together. They were each being reared by grandparents, separate sets of grandparents because they had different fathers. They didn't know where their mother was. Neither of them had much contact with their fathers, either. "But we get to see each *other* sometimes—not too much, just once in a while. And he just told me this. Last time we were together, he *told* me. I don't even know why he thought of telling me. But I couldn't believe it. He says this happens to him, like, all the time, and it made me cry so hard when he told me, because it's been happening to me all this time and I was always afraid to tell anyone, but then I got to tell him."

"There's nothing to be afraid of," Grace said, kindly—but I thought: *there is.* For this little girl, there was. Not of the symptom, maybe. But of so much—everything—else.

Before we separated in the mess hall, I gave in to my impulse to hug her, finally, and although she looked surprised, she hugged me right back, and when I let go of her, she was smiling, shyly. It was the first time I'd seen her smile. After that, for the rest of the weekend, I hugged her whenever I saw her—hugged her hello, and hugged her goodbye for good measure, too—and she didn't look surprised after the first time, and with each hug she offered up another sweet, shy smile, but after that one conversation she returned to her silence, except for singing.

I couldn't stop thinking about what she had told us, even as I sat in my corner during rehearsals and pretended to read as I listened to the solfege the girls were being taught, silently practicing the syllables in my head (*du* instead of *do*; *ri* instead of *re*—purer sounds, they were told, and it was true: the sounds were pure—the purest sounds, I thought, I'd ever heard).

The next morning, Grace greeted me breathlessly. Before bedtime, when the girls in the Santa Maria cabin sat in a circle again, talking, she had told them all about the extraordinary conversation we had had that morning. Evidently I wasn't the only one who'd been thinking about it, puzzling over it, all day. "I didn't tell them her name," she assured me, though I hadn't asked, "just that she was in Pinta. But then I don't even remember her name, so I guess I couldn't have anyway" (already she had the makings of a fine memoirist herself). "Anyway, it was amazing. Are you ready for this? *Two* girls in my cabin said they have it too. For years. And neither of *them* had ever told anybody before, either."

I must have looked skeptical—mightn't they not have chimed in because this sounded so interesting, and they wanted to be interesting, too?—because Grace said, "I'm *serious*, Mama. Really, you should have seen the way they looked when I started talking about it. And then they both started talking really fast, both of them at the same time, describing how it was when it happened to them. And it was *exactly* like what happens to me. None of us could believe it—we just kept looking at each other, like, 'I can't believe this happens to *you*, too.'"

"What did the other girls say? And the mothers, the chaperones?"

"Nobody *said* anything. They just looked at us. I'm sure they all thought *we* were all just weird." Grace was used to being called weird. She had recently decided to think of it as a compliment, which seemed to have worked: she had tricked herself into not minding it.

At home, late Sunday night, I typed *smaller, bigger, far away, near, visual, illusion, hallucination*, and so on—in various combinations, with and without quotation marks ("small and far away")—into Google. Why hadn't I thought of doing this years ago? I wondered. Why had I taken the experts at their word? Had I been so relieved that there was nothing "truly terrible" wrong with her that I saw no reason to pursue it? Or had I—a darker thought—been so in love with the idea of Grace as a complete original (my precocious, creative daughter! She writes, she acts, she sings, she dances—and she invents entirely original symptoms!) that I'd had no interest in finding out otherwise?

After the usual number of fruitless hits, I struck paydirt. I learned that these visual illusions are called *metamorphosias*, and that the particular types of *metamorphosias* to which Grace (and the other Santa Marias, and the Pinta and her brother) were subject were called *micropsia* accompanied by *teleopsia* (objects are seen as "minified" and at the same time far away) and *macropsia* accompanied by *pelopsia* (large and close). "The condition"—this sentence was repeated word for word on site after site (health sites, science sites, encyclopedia and dictionary sites)—"is in terms of perception only; the mechanics of the eye are not affected, only the brain's interpretation of information passed from the eyes."

The syndrome (the two extremes seemed always to be paired, to create a single "syndrome") was common enough to have a common name, a slang name: *Alice in Wonderland Syndrome*. There was nearly always a connection to migraines, as Grace's pediatrician had suggested, and this explained the phenomenon's common name, for Lewis Carroll was "known to have suffered from migraines"—once again, the same line appeared unaltered in hundreds of sites—and "there is some speculation that he might have written that work from direct experience."

I wanted to look in the choir roster and call the girls and ask about migraines—but I restrained myself. It wasn't any of my business, after all; I had no right. And certainly if they weren't telling their families, it wasn't appropriate for me to—not when we were talking about something that didn't endanger them. So instead of picking up the phone, I did what I always do when something is nagging at the corners of my mind. I made notes. Vaguely, I thought I might make use of them for an essay someday, although when I mentioned this to Grace, she said, "It sounds more like a science fair project than one of your essays"—and then, before I could suggest that she consider making it *her* next science fair project (because when she said this, it suddenly struck me as a terrific idea), she held up one hand (she knows me *very* well) and said, "Don't even *think* about it, Mama."

In truth, it seemed less like a potential essay *or* a science fair project than a brainteaser, the kind of problem Grace's fourth grade teacher used to put on the board every morning—a puzzling anecdote that had some trick hidden inside it that had to be teased out in order to solve the problem it posed (*the truck driver heads south on a one-way northbound street, but is not stopped by the policeman on the corner, who waves and smiles at him as he makes the turn* [answer: the truck driver is not in his truck at the time; he is on foot]).

Seven months passed. According to my notes, which I continued to make whenever anything of interest occurred, or occurred to me, relating to Getting-Smaller-and-Getting-Bigger (I couldn't substitute the nickname I'd found on the Internet for the one we'd created; we'd been using ours for too long—and besides, it was *ours*), during this period Grace experienced GSAGB only once. I turned my attention to fiction. Then, in early April, I was at a writers' conference in Vancouver, sitting at a large round table eating breakfast with friends I rarely see. The friend sitting on my right side asked what I was working on these days, and I talked about the novella I was rethinking as a novel—and then, because he is an essayist himself, I mentioned that I'd also been making notes, on and off, toward a new essay I couldn't get a handle on, something I wasn't sure would ever amount to anything. Before I knew it, I found myself telling him, and everyone else at the table, about Grace's hallucinations and what had happened at the choir retreat. My friend said, "You're not serious." And here it was again—my friend Joe, a writer, editor, and teacher, a man a few years younger than I—had experienced exactly the same kind of hallucination "regularly—and often. I mean, a *lot*" all through his childhood. He hadn't thought about it in years, he said. And he had never mentioned it to a soul until now. "I can't believe this," he said. He said this again and again.

"Why didn't you tell anyone?" I asked him.

"Are you joking? I was eight or nine when it started. I figured that either, *a*) this was the way *everyone* saw the world, and they would think I was crazy for bothering to mention it, or *b*) I was the *only* one who saw things this way—in which case they would think I was crazy. Either way, I was crazy."

"It didn't occur to you that anyone would be sympathetic, or worried about you? That they'd want to find out why this was happening to you?"

"Not until this second." He crumpled up his napkin, tossed it onto his empty plate. "Too late now, huh?" And then he laughed. "But really, you don't know my family."

When I got back to Columbus, I composed an e-mail and posted it on the listserv for writers at Ohio State, the easiest way for me to reach hundreds of people at once (or anyway, hundreds of people who are likely to answer if I ask a question). I described the phenomenon of GSAGB and asked if anyone reading the message had ever experienced anything similar.

The creative writing listserv goes out to current MFA students and faculty, undergraduate writers, alumni of the MFA program who want to stay in touch, English department undergrad alumni writers, and a substantial number of local writers whose only involvement with the university *is* our listserv. After I hit "send," I thought for a moment—nothing but writers, really?—then decided to cast the net a little wider, as long as I was in listserv-posting mode. I sent the same note to a smaller listserv I maintain myself, of graduate student artists in other fields (dance, music composition, painting and sculpture, theater) who have ever taken a course with me, and then—what the hell, I thought—to the English department's all-faculty listserv.

I got the first response within the hour, and over the next few days, every time I checked my e-mail, there was something in my inbox—more often, several things—in response to my post. Every one of them expressed surprise, even shock, about being asked about this. *I thought it was just me* (often punctuated by an exclamation point) was the phrase that turned up most often, and nearly every e-mail included the lines *I haven't thought about this in years* and *I've never talked about this to anyone.*

By the time the responses stopped coming, I had heard from twenty-four people who had experienced Getting-Smaller-and-Getting-Bigger (not a single one of them called it Alice in Wonderland Syndrome; none of them seemed to have a name for it at all) or else just Getting-Smaller (and far away). (No one reported *only* Getting-Bigger/closer.) I wrote back to everyone who'd written to me, not only to thank them but to ask about migraines. There were no migraine sufferers among them. In fact, the only thing most of my respondents had in common—besides being literary or artistic, which was a given, considering the population of the various listservs addressed—was that they all seemed to have been considered, and thus to have considered themselves, "weird kids" (and, like Grace, they seemed mostly to have learned early to claim their "weirdness" as a positive mark of distinction). They offered up this information without my asking, as if to *them* it was a possible explanation.

Only two had ever told anyone about their hallucinations. One of them, a newly minted PhD in cultural studies from my department, had told his doctors, because he had cerebral palsy, and thought—as did the doctors when he told them—that this was "just another symptom" (albeit one that had not been documented) of the CP. *And of course it's possible that it was,* he wrote. *How could I know, even now?*

The other was an even more unusual case (Grace was right; I was

starting to think of this as a science fair project): a colleague—a literary critic whose fields were modernism, feminist literary theory, and
neuroscience and language—who said that *all* of her "episodes," as
she scrupulously called them, had taken place in her late teens or early
twenties, and who had talked about the experience in her classes, because it seemed relevant "especially when teaching poetry or some of
the more difficult modernist texts." The episode she considered "the
most notable" occurred when she returned from the hospital after the
birth of her first child.

> *In those days (1959) the hospital stay was one week and culminated with a lob-
> ster dinner. The test for going home was the ability to sit on one's episiotomy for
> the time it took to consume the lobster. I was nineteen, (hastily) married, still
> in school. My parents were waiting in the living room of my apartment. When
> I entered, my mother unceremoniously swept my daughter from my arms and
> retreated to the sofa, where she and my father, first-time grandparents, kvelled
> over the baby. Though the room was small, I experienced the three of them as
> very far away—and when I say far away, I mean the (perversely constituted,
> secular) trinity appeared to be tiny figures, the length of the room stretched by a
> good hundred feet.*

She had been a "much indulged first child," she went on to say.
She had nearly died before she was a year old, she explained, and as a
result, her "parents had dedicated their lives to me; my brother to this
day has never forgiven me for the superior attentions." At the moment that she saw her own first child and her parents together "at the
wrong end of the telescope," she felt she was being given a glimpse
of something about adult life, and about motherhood. "It was as if I
were literally being *shown* something," she said, "with respect to the
centrality of a luxuriously selfish child and her new autonomy (for
better *and* worse—though at that moment, it was simply terrifying)."

After that, when it happened again—as always, suddenly, unexpectedly (though less terrifyingly with repetition)—it seemed clear to
her that the symptom was announcing her "ambivalence of the moment and seemed always to involve in some way a sobering lesson
about my own power of autonomy."

Most of the people who wrote to me had "outgrown" their hallucinations, they said, with adolescence, but a few had had them since
childhood, into their teens and twenties (and they were still in their

twenties now). A few, like the feminist critic, reported an onset in their teens. One of my graduate students, a woman nearing thirty, told me she had been "plagued by" the phenomenon as a child but that it still happened occasionally, "when I'm being interviewed for a job, say—you know, when I'm in a situation where I'm nervous and feel I'm being judged. Well, when I *am* being judged, I guess."

Another graduate student said that it "was quite overwhelming as a physical experience [and] it happened only at night when I was alone. . . . I'd be lying in bed in the dark, looking at the thin strip of light from the closet and feeling a complete loss of control. At the same time, it was sort of comforting after a while because it was predictable and kind of muffling. It felt like being surrounded by cotton, as if my head was getting huge and then shrinking down to a pinprick . . . and I also had the impression that my skin was becoming completely porous, that in the midst of all this shrinking and expanding, my skin was just disintegrating." But even though she was afraid, she went on, she didn't feel *anxious.* "At the time, it felt like the opposite of anxiety or panic: very slow and silent, like being buried in a snow drift."

This made me think of a short story by Conrad Aiken, "Silent Snow, Secret Snow," which I have always loved, and which I used to teach (I stopped years ago, because I discovered that my students found it "creepy"—they thought of it as a horror story, which I have since discovered *is* the way it is usually classified—while I have always found it "merely" profoundly heart-wrenching). It's a story in which a child is experiencing something no one else is aware of, and snow is Aiken's metaphor, just as it was my MFA student's, in her e-mail. When I wrote back to her, with the usual thank you and the question about migraines, I also asked if she knew the Aiken story; she didn't. The next day, I put a photocopy of it in her mailbox, with a note in which I conceded that many people considered it to be a horror story, that I did not, but that I had long ago given up trying to persuade people who saw it as "creepy" that I was right. That I hoped she would see why I had passed it along to her.

(I am not a very good teacher of literature, since I learned early on that I can't persuade anyone to my point of view about a given story. And also that I don't really want to persuade them. I am a much better writing teacher. This doesn't stop me, however, from giving my students many things to read, both in and out of my classroom.

I just *give* them the stuff, though, and hope for the best. If it's a piece of writing I love, I will sometimes tell them why, but I no longer expect them to love it, too. Not even when it's just one story given to one particular writing student, like this time. And she never said a word to me about it, so I suppose she did find it more horrifying than heartbreaking—or else that she simply didn't like it.)

After a while, I stopped being surprised that these children (for all but a few who responded had experienced this in childhood, if not in childhood only) hadn't told their parents or anyone else about what they were experiencing, even though they knew (as the student of mine who had felt herself being buried in snow said she always knew, "as a sort of edge around the silence, and the calm") that this "wasn't supposed to happen, this [couldn't] be normal"—mostly because they were always so surprised that I would imagine they *would* have told. I felt naïve in the face of *their* surprise. I'd had no idea that children as a rule were so secretive. The only secrets I can remember keeping from my parents as a child were some of the stories I wrote—because I knew they'd *ooh* and *ah* over them without paying attention to whether they were any good or not—and the bad news that my fourth grade teacher hated me and was making my life a misery. Otherwise I wanted to tell them everything. The only obstacle to this was their refusal or inability to listen to some of what I wanted to say.

Perhaps this is one reason the Aiken story broke my heart when I first read it. The child who cannot tell, who knows no one will understand—this was what I, throughout my childhood, most wanted *not* to be.

I didn't start keeping secrets in earnest until I was a teenager, when suddenly everything became a secret, and I felt every bit as alone as I had always feared I was.

4

If this *had* been a science fair project, I would have lost points for the small, haphazard sample, and for my exclusive concentration on literary and artistic types. (I knew this because I was one of the judges — by dint of an undergraduate degree in chemistry, a subject about which I remembered almost nothing — at the science fair at Grace's school, and I was always very strict about sample size and range.) But now that I knew that the symptom I had been assured was so unusual was *not* unusual (even if it was — and for all I knew, it *was* — mostly limited to "creative" people), it seemed to me I had no choice but to go on a search for more information. And when I want to *really* know something, I tend to turn off the computer and turn to books, and to people. My first stop was a conversation with my physician friend, a neuro-ophthalmologist who teaches in the medical school at Ohio State.

Steve Katz is a physician with a literary bent, and when we talk (which is not very often, and never for very long, because neither of us has any free time), it is usually about novels or poetry. This time, I had warned him, I wanted to grill him about Alice in Wonderland Syndrome.

We met at Cup O' Joe, a Columbus institution, at a small square table surrounded by young people and their laptops. As soon as I sat down, I took out a notebook. I should have felt like a journalist, but I felt like an undergraduate. Steve had brought his briefcase, from which he pulled a stack of journal articles. He set them on the table between us.

"Just some background," he said.

"Thanks." I glanced at the first page of the topmost article. It had diagrams. I couldn't remember the last time I'd read anything with diagrams. "That's great," I said. "So" — pen poised — "tell me: how often have you actually encountered micropsia and macropsia in your practice?"

"Often," he said.

I set my pen down. "Really?"

"Why is that so surprising?"

"Because I thought it was considered rare."

"Oh, I wouldn't say that. I see it often enough, at any rate, so that it doesn't surprise me when I do." He took a sip of his vanilla latte and waited to see if I were going to pick up my pen again and write this down. I did.

"So it's *not* uncommon, then," I said.

"Well, no, I wouldn't say that, either. But you have to remember that I almost never see anyone with a 'common' complaint. I mean, nobody just picks himself up and goes to see a neuro-ophthalmologist. Somebody sends him. So I'm the last guy a patient sees, not the first. That means that unless a problem is fairly unusual, I don't run into it at all. It also means that by the time that patient gets to me, every obvious cause has already been ruled out."

"And the obvious causes of something like this? What would those be?"

"Well, let's see." Steve settled in comfortably, both hands around his mug. He looked happy and relaxed—two ways I was pretty sure I'd never seen him look before—and it struck me that this was the first time we'd ever had a conversation in which he got to be the expert and I the willing student. "First," he said, "you want to look at whether it's macular—an eye problem. And you can tell right away if that's what's going on, because if it's macular, it's constant. It doesn't come and go the way it does for Grace and all these other people you've been hearing from."

"Wait," I said, "are you telling me that there are people who walk around seeing the world this way all the time? Seeing things smaller and larger than they really are? But how is that possible? How do they manage?"

"Actually, when it's macular, it's one way or the other—micropsia or macropsia, not both. And people who have it aren't even aware of it, usually. Not from the start, anyway. It's generally just in one eye, so the other eye compensates, making things look normal. It's only in certain situations—say, when the lighting is dim—that the deformation even becomes noticeable. That's what sends people to their ophthalmologists."

"So that's what Grace's ophthalmologist was looking for? Evidence of some kind of macular . . . what?"

"Edema, or a macular hole. Some kind of dysfunction. If there's nothing like that going on, then it's not an eye problem, so you want to find out if it's a brain problem. So the next step is an MRI—"

"Or a CAT scan?

"Is that what Grace's doctor ordered? That's fine. An MRI is a little better for this, but if there'd been anything to see, the CT scan would have shown it." He studied me for a second. "Really. A CT would definitely have been sufficient. Stop worrying."

It occurred to me that he must be an unusually sensitive doctor.

"Okay," Steve said. "The next thing we look for are other indications of a pre-migraine syndrome. Because, as Grace's doctor told you, this is often a precursor to migraines. If there are no other indications of migraine, and no history of migraines in the family, one of two things happen. Sometimes you'll see a patient with Alice in Wonderland Syndrome, and the vision is normal and nothing turns up on an MRI, but there's no migraine history—like with Grace, as you've indicated—and then years later they do develop migraines and you say, 'Oops, I missed that one, didn't I?'"

"And the other outcome? Because none of the people who responded to my e-mail survey were under twenty-five, and some of them were over fifty, and none of them had migraines. Presumably, if they were going to develop them, they would have by now, right?"

"Probably." Steve drummed his fingers on the table. Then he stopped abruptly. "Oh! By the way, I wanted to tell you: that's what the literary reference is about. It's not just an allusion to the DRINK ME and EAT ME in the Alice story—"

"I know all about Lewis Carroll and his migraines," I said. And then added, "Sorry," because he looked so disappointed. I should have just let him tell me. "I Googled," I told him. "I wouldn't have known otherwise. But what about the other one?"

"The other one of what?"

"The other outcome," I reminded him. "You said, 'One of two things happen,' and you said, 'Sometimes years later they do develop migraines after all.' So . . . ?"

"So nothing," he said, just as Dr. Sheets had, years before. *You want to know where we go from here, but there's nowhere to go from here.*

"That's the other possibility? Migraine or nothing?"

"Well, we don't say 'nothing.' We'd have to consider all those cases idiopathic. Which means—"

"I know what it means," I said, interrupting him again. This time I didn't apologize. "It just means you don't know what the hell it is."

"That's what it means, yes."

"So do you actually tell your patients that?"

"Not in so many words," he said. Now he looked glum.

I myself was feeling pretty good all of a sudden. It wasn't that I was happy that Steve didn't have any answers for me—at least I don't think it was. I hadn't expected answers. I'd only wanted to know what his experience of metamorphosias—the experience of someone who was an expert in vision *and* the brain—had been. But I was also enjoying the turnabout between us, I understood. You can't have a proper friendship with someone when you're the one who's considered to have superior knowledge, or whose opinions have more weight (and then, when he asks you something you *don't* know the answer to, he is so surprised and disappointed because you're supposed to be the expert). It was awfully nice for us to have swapped positions in every way.

"You know what bothers me about the 'diagnosis' *idiopathic*?" I asked him.

"Probably. People hate it when doctors don't have an answer."

"No, that's not it."

Steve squinted at me. "Really? You don't *like* it, do you?"

I smiled. "No. I'm like everyone else: I want doctors to have answers. But I understand perfectly that sometimes—often, actually—they don't. No, what bothers me about 'idiopathic' as a diagnosis is that it covers too much ground. It's so *vague*. I mean, anything that doesn't have a clear-cut, concrete, physiological cause just gets dumped into that same category. It's so . . . sloppy."

"I suppose." Now he *sounded* glum, too.

I patted his hand. "As a guy who likes to read poetry, you must have a hard time some days fitting into the world of everything's-concrete. It's a pretty literal-minded crowd you travel with."

"You have no idea," he said.

We were both silent for a moment. Finally I said, "You know, really, it's weird. Even Alice ate something and drank something — talk about concrete causes! — to make it happen to her. And what did happen to her was *so* concrete: *she* became big and then small, which was what made everything around her look smaller, then bigger. Lewis Carroll must have been a pretty literal-minded guy himself." I couldn't tell if this was cheering Steve up or not, but I was on a roll. "You know, I bet *making* it so concrete, in a story, made him feel better about what must have been awfully scary when it happened to him — because *he* wouldn't have known that his hallucinations were related to his migraines, would he? He would have thought of the whole ordeal as 'idiopathic' himself, and so he came up with a story about it that was soothing, in a way — that must have made it manageable for him to think about."

"I think you're reading too much into it," Steve said.

This made me laugh. "*You* have no idea."

As I said — a nice balance. Expertise — and no idea — on both sides.

And lack of expertise, paired with plenty of ideas, too.

That's what I was thinking about when I left Steve Katz that day — that combination of knowing little and having theories and opinions about much. Because that diagnosis of "idiopathic," I was thinking as I headed home with my notebook and the stack of journal articles, was itself of great interest to me. *Unknown or obscure?* That's my specialty! Any of my students could tell you that.

And here was something truly obscure, utterly unknown to me: how was it possible, I asked myself for the first time, that the metaphor of Getting-Smaller-and-Getting-Bigger had been reproduced by all these people to manifest what must have been a variety of things — different types of ambivalence, or conflict (or "simple" anxiety)? How was it possible that all of these people had independently reinvented the wheel — all of them without conscious awareness, without *knowing* (that is to say, *unconsciously*), making use of exactly the same kind of visual experience to symbolize something they were feeling? How and why would, *could*, the same metaphor be created by so many different minds? (And most of them in childhood, no less.)

How, for that matter — and this too I'd never thought to ask myself before—is it that we (or our "unconscious minds") make such metaphors at all?

If I'd staked my life on the belief that this was how human beings managed the world, I thought, how was it that I'd never paused to wonder *how* we do that?

I had paddled my way into very deep water, I realized.

There are certain ideas I have held close for so long I cannot remember a time when I didn't have them. Like the unshakable religious convictions of some of the people I most admire or love (and in some cases both), these ideas about how the world works—how *we* work—have so shaped my life, so thoroughly informed the way I experience the world, and so animated my life's *work*, I cannot imagine living without them. And like religious faith, mine has been a faith founded on deeply *felt* conviction—for the existence of an unconscious that produces metaphors ("symptoms") that ask others to see things in precisely the way the "author" of them sees things is as impossible to prove as the existence of God—and the lack of provability is no more an obstacle to me than it is to any of the faithful. I know what I know.

Yet, as I delved deeper into the meaning of Grace's newest symptom, I found myself wandering into science—the land of the provable.

How, I wanted to know, had my daughter, without any conscious awareness, seized on the metaphor of my becoming tiny and far away to represent (if indeed that was, as I theorized, what it represented) her desire to make me less significant and less central in her world? How did the part of her brain that works on vision get the message from the part of her brain that experiences emotions and thoughts ("thoughts" that she was not even aware of thinking, feelings she wasn't aware she was feeling) and act on that to make this palpable?

Or, to go back in time, how did her fear of growing up and being fully separate from me—losing me (as it must have seemed to her)—and her *longing* to separate from me and become fully herself (along with her rage at my inability to allow her to do that) work their way to the surface as a series of metaphors: the holding on to trash, the making things come out even, and so on? And when her unconscious was hard at work struggling with the crisis of separation and loss, growing up and independence, how did that translate to the *physical* act of being unable to throw away a candy wrapper after she had eaten the candy? (And when that didn't work—when that metaphor proved insufficient to reveal the secret that needed to be uncovered—how did her unconscious soon step things up a notch, so that if she even *saw* a candy wrapper someone else had dropped, she had to bend down and pick it up, hide it, keep it forever?)

She didn't know why she was doing what she was doing, but somehow she was compelled to do it, to act out the metaphor created for her (to reveal her secrets) by her unconscious. What I wanted to crack open was that *somehow*.

Or—to take a much simpler example—how does one's unconscious "make" someone accidentally leave behind a jacket at the home of somebody one would like to see again? (For in this post-Freudian age, haven't many of us had this experience, analyzed thus? *I've left my jacket behind. Oh! That must mean I want an excuse to go back there!*) But if one didn't know, at the time of leaving the jacket behind, that one was concocting an excuse—if, as we modernists assume, it was one's unconscious mind's "acting" on one's behalf—revealing, to return to Adam Phillips, a secret wish (if we are to consider the accidental leaving-behind of a jacket in the service of one's unconscious a "symptom" that can be interpreted)—how did this actually *work*? How did the author of the act guide us to do its bidding? What was the path from the meaning to the metaphor?

Surely, I thought, there was someone who knew the answer to that question.

Just because it hadn't occurred to *me* to ask it before didn't mean that others hadn't been working on an answer—for years, perhaps. Scientists. *Experts*.

I knew I wouldn't find the answer in psychoanalysis, which is dedicated to interpreting metaphors as they appear, and working on the problems expressed by them—a complex and difficult enough process all by itself. For the question of how one moves from cause to symptom—how we move from "problems" to the metaphors that have the potential to expose them, if they are looked at closely enough; for the question of how the unconscious makes its choices—why *this* metaphor to exhibit this particular meaning, and not *that* one?—I had to turn to neuroscience.

Which I did with trepidation. Most neuroscientists, I knew from my reading—and as I read further, my heart sank deeper—are loathe to consider explanations for behavior or perception that are lodged in the slippery, "soft science" of psychoanalysis, or the notion of a *self*. And what else do we mean when we invoke the word *unconscious*? The question of how much of what happens in our lives is encoded in our genetic maps, and at least theoretically traceable to something physical—even if it's a complex, unseen, *unseeable* something—was not one I wanted to debate. Or could debate effectively, even if I wanted to, for despite the degree I earned three decades ago, I can't pass even briefly, in the tiniest way, for a scientist. Even all those years ago, wearing my white lab coat and pouring benzene into an Erlenmeyer flask, I couldn't. (All I was even then was a girl who thought she'd emulate Chekhov and grow up to be a writer *and* a doctor, until I found out that I had no particular aptitude for science—with the notable exception of organic nomenclature—*and* that med school would have taken up all my writing time even if I had been able to get in, which I never would have anyway, considering my science grades. And then somewhere along the way I found out that Chekhov was *not* a writer supporting himself by practicing medicine, but vice versa—so I gladly, and with great relief, abandoned the whole venture.)

The questions I'd conceived had placed me squarely in limbo—in a peculiar uncharted territory between psychoanalysis (which, as leisurely and speculative, inquiring, and contemplative an art as it is, had—as noted—other, more pressing fish to fry) and the world of "hard science," where it seemed unlikely that I'd find someone who wouldn't scoff at my questions.

Still, I steeled myself. I kept reading, and I made inquiries. And after any number of wrong turns, ignored e-mails, and curt responses (the most sympathetic was, "Sorry—your questions are not currently answerable"), I found a neuroscientist who was willing to visit with me in the limbo of my own devising. A neurobiologist named Paul Grobstein, who had written an article called "Making the Unconscious Conscious, and Vice Versa" (more diagrams!), would be happy to entertain my questions, he said. "'How does unconscious impulse create metaphor' is . . . a REALLY interesting question [and] it's not that there aren't a variety of relevant stories with possible answers . . . but rather that, to my mind at least, none of them have proven to be sufficiently generative to be satisfying in the long run," he wrote in his first e-mail.

This was just another way of saying "sorry—questions not currently answerable," but the difference was that Grobstein was willing—and even wanted—to talk more about those questions. He wasn't surprised to hear, he said, "that so many people would report, when prompted, that they have in fact had the micropsia/macropsia experience (just as it's not particularly surprising that . . . many people are afraid of snakes, others of spiders)." There was even an "easy answer" to that part of the question, for "at the level of the brain, everyone is 'sort of the same and also sort of different' (a phrase I use in teaching)." Indeed, he added, "people actually tend to be more similar in the material out of which they make stories than they are in the stories they tell."

The *material out of which they make stories* was so much like one of the phrases I use in *my* teaching—along with "the experience of the experience" (and no doubt there are others I invoke just as often, without even being aware of it)—it stopped me in my tracks. It seemed so improbable that the novelist and the neurobiologist would employ the same terms. When I remarked on this, Grobstein said he would "gladly accept [me] into the realm of scientists" as long as I would likewise welcome him "into the world of storytellers."

There it was: that balancing of expertise again, so irresistible to me.

But expertise, I was beginning to understand, could take us only so far in this mission. For it seems that the process by which our minds work to make something happen without our being what we call "conscious" of so doing is one of the great mysteries, as yet unpenetrated by science. And it seems too that there are so many lesser mysteries to keep us busy—if we're of a mind to keep ourselves busy pondering mysteries—that this great one is not at the very top of anyone's to-do list. Freud got us started on the science (or the art—take your pick) of psychoanalysis, but the idea that our behavior is influenced by feelings of which we are unaware did not begin with Freud. In Henri Ellenberger's ambitious account of the history of psychotherapy, *The Discovery of the Unconscious*, he notes that "the assumption that a part of psychic life escapes man's conscious knowledge" was held for centuries before Freud codified it. And the idea that we feel and do things we cannot understand or explain goes back at least as far as Pascal: "The heart has its reasons of which reason knows nothing."

Indeed, this makes instinctive sense to most of us—but even if we believe this, even if we sense that we have feelings we can't readily access, even if we feel certain there are "unconscious motivations" behind much of what we do, the question of how this works (how one leads to another) is not the one that generally occupies us.

But then we don't live in an age that has much patience for pondering such questions. We want things to work, and never mind how they do. As far as I can tell, the entire "psychotherapeutic" drug industry is based on this line of thinking. While I myself imagine psychotropic medications—for example, the newer antidepressants, selective serotonin reuptake inhibitors (SSRIs) such as Zoloft and Prozac, which by now have been taken by upward of twenty million people in the United States alone—as providing a sort of blockade between the unconscious (which is working to create a symbol for what is being experienced by the person housing that particular unconscious) and the rest of that person's self (the body, the nervous system, behavior—everything, that is, beyond one's unconscious), the truth is that no one *knows* exactly how they work. For the three percent of the population of the United States (or eight million people) who exhibit obsessive-compulsive behavior, SSRIs very often *do* work—at least as long as the patient keeps taking the medicine—to prevent the behavior that is so disruptive, but without anyone understanding why.

That there is a continuous process within each of us that records and makes use of everything we experience, and transforms it without our conscious minds' awareness—that makes us behave as we do, and brings us dreams, and "psychogenic" symptoms, and the inspiration for art—is such a preposterous idea that it's amazing, really, that any of us believe in it at all. But most of us do. Most of us believe in a "self"—a complex, invisible package that is unique—and even a child, when presented with the Freudian notion of an "accident" that provides information about the unconscious (an object left behind, a slip of the tongue), not only grasps it but delights in it (the complexities of one's own mind!). But because it is impossible to directly deal with the unconscious, we are left to speculate—and only speculate—about what it's up to *and* how it works.

Because of that reliance on speculation, there is an army—beyond the borders of neuroscience—of *non*believers: a small but insistent army who live by the credo of If-I-Can't-See-It-Obviously-It-Doesn't-Exist who have dismissed Freud entirely. Who would scoff at my determination to place Grace's hallucination in a metaphorical context. Who mock the soft science (who hoot at anyone's use of the word "science" in this context) of psychoanalysis as practiced by any post-Freudian psychotherapists. Who believe that the notion of the unconscious is nothing more than a "culturally supported myth."

Among the most passionate nonbelievers of our time are the former literary critic Frederick Crews, who now positions himself as a "metacritic" (writing criticism of criticism) and anti-Freudian; the philosopher Adolf Grünbaum, at the University of Pittsburgh; and the classical philologist Sebastiano Timpanaro (who, until his death in 2000, supported himself as a proofreader—he was too shy to hold a teaching position—although, like most of the anti-unconscious camp, he was a sort of contemporary Renaissance man: a historian of textual criticism, an authority on early nineteenth century Italian cultural history, and a well-known political theorist of the revolutionary Italian left, as well as a Freud-debunker). But they are by no means the only ones.

Richard Webster, whose education was in English literature but who has become a professional anti-Freudian, insists that anyone who would argue with him about the veracity of psychoanalysis is missing the point. In the paperback edition of *Why Freud Was Wrong*, he addresses those who reviewed the hardcover edition of the book negatively:

> *One of the arguments deployed . . . suggested that to portray psychoanalysis as a false science, as I do in this book, is to misunderstand its nature. According to this view the whole point of psychoanalysis is that it is not a science at all; it should be judged not as a contribution to our systematic knowledge of human nature but as a kind of poetry. Psychoanalytic theories, therefore, can never be rejected as "false" . . . [a] view of Freud [that] is certainly seductive. For by elegantly dissolving the truth-claims which are everywhere apparent in psycho-*

analysis it makes it possible to evade the task of evaluating Freud's theories critically.

Robert T. Carroll, who teaches philosophy and maintains a debunker's website, www.skepdic.com, is blunter:

> *To those whose lives are devoted to getting into the unconscious mind, either to find out why they have problems or to find some transcendent truth, I say you will be looking for a long, long time. You might better spend your time reading a book on memory or neuroscience.*

In other words: Trust to science. Consult the experts.

5

But there are, it turns out, no experts when it comes to the way our minds work. It turns out that your guess really is as good as mine — or as good as a neurobiologist's.

The neurobiologist Paul Grobstein's ideas about how unconsciousness and consciousness work together are based on the principle that the human brain is "bipartite," by which he means not only that "there is a meaningful distinction between 'conscious' and 'unconscious' aspects of its structure/function" but also that "since consciousness is a part of the brain which is in turn a part of the body, consciousness has no direct information about either the world or the body, [so] whatever information it has about these things is acquired indirectly from the rest of the nervous system (the unconscious part)."

He defines the unconscious as "consisting of a large number of different semi-isolated modules, each interacting with the body and through it the outside world in its own distinctive ways. It is the reports of these modules (and only the reports of these modules) that reach 'consciousness' and it is the distinct task of 'consciousness' to make sense of these reports, i.e., to come up with a story that accounts for them."

For Grobstein, "this is what consciousness does. It is what 'consciousness' *is* in the most fundamental way. It is a storyteller that tries to make sense of the cacophony of signals it receives from the unconscious. And everything that we actually experience (perceptions, thoughts, feelings, intentions . . . in contrast to the many things that happen to us or [that] we do without being aware of it) [is] the product of this storytelling process. In short, consciousness is 'story' . . . a way of making sense of things (that might always be made sense of in other ways) which in turn generates new questions/observations/stories."

Metaphor, he says, is "just one of the tricks that is used (along with 'meaning' and 'time' and 'causation,' among other things) to bring order to the cacophony of signals. . . . The upshot is that one actually has, at all times, two influences on one's behavior: the multiplex state of the unconscious and the current more or less coherent 'story' that reflects an attempt to give coherence to that. One may, at any given time, behave in terms of the unconscious or in terms of the story or in terms of some combination of the two, [and] there is, I think, not great mystery about this, though many people are still not entirely comfortable with the degree to which behavior reflects the unconscious."

The "many people" Grobstein speaks of here must refer to his fellow and sister scientists—gentlefolk all (clearly Grobstein has not been reading the professional debunkers, who all seem to be very angry, rather than "not entirely comfortable").

Where Grobstein—like virtually all neuroscientists, and many psychologists and contemporary psychiatrists as well—is in agreement with the philosophers, literary critics, and professional skeptics who have devoted themselves to discrediting psychoanalytic theory is in his rejection of the notion of "repression" that is basic to Freudian psychoanalysis. Still, Paul Grobstein is friendly to the idea of unconscious *motivation* in a way that marks him as something of a maverick in his own field. For him, there is "in general no particular problem in making sense of someone . . . exhibiting behaviors that have an origin with which the person [himself] is not familiar (e.g., a man who was abused by a red-haired woman as a child and who has trouble being comfortable with his otherwise wonderful red-haired wife)," and he appreciates "the subtlety" that is recognized by what he refers to as the "psychoanalytic storytelling tradition." That psychoanalysis asks, "Why is it that the earlier experience is not consciously accessible, i.e., part of the story?" is something Grobstein admires. But "psychoanalytic tradition would typically attribute that to 'repression' or, perhaps more meaningfully, to 'conflict,' i.e., to something that actively prevents that aspect of the experience from becoming part of the story because it . . . is unacceptable by some criterion (the abusive woman was the man's mother, and so the man would have to acknowledge his own involvement in violating a social proscription against incest?)."

Grobstein believes that this interpretation "misses some obvious things and in so doing overlooks some critical issues."

To his way of thinking, the things that happen to us happen *first* "in the unconscious and only become conscious if/when they become part of the storytelling process itself. Hence," he says, "a simpler interpretation of the behavior of the man in relation to red hair is that the things that happened to him altered one or another part of his unconscious without ever being fully reported to the storyteller"—this is the phrase Grobstein uses for what we might call the man's "conscious mind"—and rather than his having "repressed" anything, the explanation for his discomfort would be "the unconscious signaling dread in the presence of red without the storyteller having had or having any information about the events themselves." He adds that "it's worth noting [too] that the red signaling dread phenomenon could also have an explanation in genetic information, i.e., with no actual events involved at all."

For me—right up to the genetic explanation (a gene that would cause our theoretical man to be uneasy around redheads?)—this seemed to be (if you'll pardon the expression) splitting hairs. The difference between Grobstein's theory (first comes the unconscious, then the story) and psychoanalytic theory (in which, at least in Grobstein's retelling of it, "everything is story *before* it becomes unconscious") doesn't seem that significant to me. It reminds me of certain arguments among literary scholars, the "solution" to which will have no meaning to anyone other than the critics involved in the debate—and certainly not to the writers about whose work the critics are arguing. In other words, the unconscious doesn't care one way or the other: it is just going to keep on going about its business.

To Grobstein, while there is no such thing as repression, there is "the issue of what does and doesn't become part of the story, and a reciprocal exchange between the unconscious and the storytelling process that allows the constraints of storytelling to become significant not only in the final story but also in how one acts unconsciously." When he takes up my "left-behind jacket," he suggests that it would be possible that the jacket was not "left behind" at all—that is, that the meaning *left behind* did not exist until after the fact, that perhaps only after the jacket-owner's acquaintance phoned her to say, "You left your jacket here," and she returned to his house to retrieve it, did that meaning become part of the story. In Grobstein's view, we humans tend to take "a lot of disconnected things and [create] a unitary story about them. One that may or may not actually be 'true.' There are 'things' (in the darkness, not actually verbalizable) before there is 'story.'"

This is, as it happens, exactly what I mean when I talk to my students about the "raw material" of life—the *things in the darkness*. Before there is *story*.

As to Grace and the Getting-Smaller-and-Getting-Bigger, Grobstein interpreted it this way.

> *Her unconscious was reporting both worry about your closeness and worry about your increasing distance. The two reports couldn't be accommodated in a single story so they came to be expressed one at a time in two sequential experiences/stories with each report being reduced in its salience in the cacophony by their successive expression. After which the storyteller, for a time, didn't have to deal further with the conflict or its own inability to resolve it. And, with longer time, as the unconscious reshaped itself with age/experiences, the need to create stories along these lines waned.*
>
> *Is that what* actually *happened? I don't and can't know. . . . [which is the] downside to the bipartite brain story. . . . You can't know anything with certainty. . . . On the flip side, though, the bipartite brain architecture gives us the capability to conceive and try out a very large range of stories to see which ones work best in particular cases. One achieves along this path the freedom to become, and, in becoming, to be oneself the agent of new territory to explore and inquire into.*

I wasn't satisfied, exactly. The bipartite brain story wasn't an answer, after all, and an answer—something definitive and provable (with diagrams!)—was what I'd been hoping for. (Actually, it occurs to me that my hopeful belief that "science" might be able to provide such an answer may tell me something more—beyond Chekhov, that is—about why I majored in chemistry in college, despite all the evidence that it was a bad fit for me. I remember my physical chemistry teacher taking me aside and pleading with me to give it up. Professor Finston liked me and felt terrible about having to enter into his gradebook the grades I was earning. He thought it would be better if I just dropped the course, dropped the major, concentrated "on poetry, which is where I am sure you belong.")

But I was interested in the terms of Grobstein's search for an answer, and in particular the way his approach was "sort of the same and also sort of different" from mine. The storytelling aspect of his "bipartite brain" theory was startlingly like what I tell my students about how to create a character who seems to be alive and wholly real even though he "lives" only on the page. I always talk about how important it is that readers know about both "the raw material" the character encounters *and* "the story he tells himself" at any given moment about it—so that the first two questions I ask are: *What's happening right now to this character?* and *What's the story he is telling himself* about *what's happening to him* (what he's seeing, hearing, feeling, et cetera—and thinking or remembering)? But *then* I want to know, *What's the story he* imagines *he's telling himself, as opposed to the story he is "really" telling himself?* And *What's the difference between those two stories?*—for in that space, it seems to me, lies the narrative: the story being told to the reader.

To talk about the story we think we're telling ourselves versus the story we're "really" telling ourselves is another way of talking about the secrets we're not aware we're keeping—which is to say, a way of talking about the unconscious. When all three parts of an experience are in play (let's call this my tripartite theory of experience)—the "something that happens," the story we unconsciously tell ourselves about it as it happens, and the story we think we're telling ourselves about it as it happens—we are simply living our lives. It's when we stop to try to pull the three parts apart (What *was* the thing that just happened, exactly? What happened to me around it? What did I think happened to me around it? Why is there a difference between these?) that we have the chance to understand our own unconscious processes. (And when novelists consider these questions about a character, the character becomes very nearly a living, breathing human being.)

When it comes to one's own unconscious, we are all potential experts. It doesn't take much more than the willingness to plumb one's own secrets—the willingness, the interest, the patience, the belief that it's worth the time and trouble. Like all experts, we have certain methodologies, a handful of reliable tools, and eventually—if we make a habit of this sort of work—we arrive at something like a best practice. We make use of dreams and of Freud's "free associa-tion," which at least in theory provide a window to the unconscious (although it's much more difficult to associate freely, without organiz-ing or interpreting these "associations"—without, that is, telling our-selves a story—than Freud suggested); we set ourselves to the task of plain old-fashioned analysis, or self-analysis—a kind of metaphori-cal rolling up of one's shirt sleeves and getting down to the work of thinking things through. I have always been surprised by how much can be accomplished by the latter. And yet—and yet—

What surprises me even more, always, is how stubborn the uncon-scious is. How forcefully it resists our efforts, no matter how expert those efforts may be.

Like all highly qualified experts, it turns out, we can't be expert *enough*.

There will always be much more we don't know than what we do—simply because there is so much to *be* known. Dig as we may, we can unearth only so much.

Idiopathic, that word invoked so often by physicians to describe complaints they can't otherwise diagnose, despite years of education, training, experience, expertise—the word that stands in for "one of the many things—the vast, uncountable number of things—we do not, and apparently cannot, know"—is from the Greek *idiopatheia*.

From *idios*—that which pertains to the self; that which is private or separate—and *pátheia*—suffering, feeling.

I should not be surprised (and yet I am, again and again) by the *idiopatheia* of the unconscious.

By the age of seven and a half, my daughter was fully aware of her own conflict between (in her terms) wanting to stay a baby and wanting to grow up—or, as she would sometimes say, even more bluntly, "want-ing Mama and not wanting Mama." But that awareness didn't stop her unconscious from producing Getting-Smaller-and-Getting-Bigger, as if her *knowing* that she was in conflict wasn't quite enough—as if it (her unconscious, that is) *had* to make the conflict visible to her. As if that were its job, or its compulsion. Or even just its habit. (Now I've conjured up—for myself, anyway—an image of the unconscious as Mean Girl, as bully, as small-time movie-gangster, reflexively snarling, *You want me to draw you a picture?*)

Even four, five, six years later, when Grace was sure she understood what Getting-Smaller-and-Getting-Bigger meant, sure she knew *why* it happened (if not—if never—how), even long after she could possibly have had the need to have a picture drawn for her, *it still happened*. Not often (and after six years, hardly at all). Just often enough to serve as a reminder. *This isn't over yet*—that's what her unconscious seemed to be saying. *Stay vigilant. Don't get complacent.*

And just as eight years, ten years, after "the problems" with which she had so struggled at the age of six had been successfully resolved, she would still occasionally feel a flutter of anxiety over throwing something away and find herself putting it into her pocket instead.

. . . .

6

My daughter is eighteen—halfway to nineteen—as I write these last pages. Time flies on paper. Of course, times flies anywhere. It hardly seems possible that I began making notes toward this essay when she was only eleven years old, when it was still difficult for her to be away overnight. Now she is at college six hundred miles from home.

She rarely calls when she's away at school. She's too busy, she tells me—not untruthfully, but incompletely. It's too taxing, she allowed herself, just once, to admit. She and I have no small talk, and we haven't figured out yet (it's possible we never will) how to "just check in," the way people do: *hello, all's well, here's the latest news from school/from home, goodbye*. If we talk, we *talk*. And so we go for weeks, for months, not talking at all.

When she comes home for a visit, though, we talk the way we always have. It does my heart good to be reminded, listening to her talk about her life, that if she needs to try to figure something out, she knows how to do it. When I think about my accomplishments as her mother—and I do think about them, especially when she is back at school and I am missing her; it helps to buoy me up when I am feeling low—I count this among them: that at eighteen and a half, she may be as much of an expert in herself as it is possible to be.

I count accomplishments, and I count blessings, too. That she sees things, always now, at the size they really are and at the distance from her that they really are. That like the other symptoms/metaphors that plagued her longer ago than Getting-Smaller-and-Getting-Bigger (the trash saving and the "catching up," the need to make things come out even, the compulsive stream-of-consciousness monologizing), this one lost its usefulness as a way to express a truth about herself to herself—or even just to remind her that a battle might not be quite over, to whisper *don't forget*.

And while I sometimes pine for the sound of her voice when

she's away at school, busy with her theater and psychology classes, her work-study job at a children's theater, her rehearsals, her friends, and everything else—I also celebrate, daily, in private, the triumph that her not-calling represents. That she doesn't need to tell me everything she's doing, everything that's on her mind. That she's living her life. *Idios.*

Don't get me wrong. I don't mean that my daughter is not capable of kidding herself. I don't mean that she—that anyone—can have it all figured out, can be immune to the guiding hand of her own unconscious. I don't even mean that I'd *want* her to be, if I had a say in it. So much of the joy—and so much of the art—of a life fully lived comes to us through what *isn't* conscious choice or action, through what seems to choose us. When someone says he never felt he'd made a choice—about whom to love, or about his occupation ("I didn't choose to be a writer, it was simply what I *was*," or, more solemnly, "*It* chose *me*")—he's talking about the unconscious forces that shape us.

For better or for worse.

I thought about this after a telephone conversation with an old friend, a conversation that made me shake my head (in pity, in wonder). The friend is someone of whom I am deeply fond, although we haven't seen each other in many years—although, in fact, we rarely talk anymore, even on the phone.

Because she is a decade younger than I and was still in college when we met, I continue to think of her as "young," despite the fact that she is middle aged herself now. Just as I continue to think of her as a close friend, even though we hardly ever talk, even though she lives eight hundred miles away. But we used to live in the same town. For two years when I first knew her, and then for two years somewhere else, we lived in the same town and saw each other nearly every day. And for those four years, and the years between the two pairs of years—and all the years since (more than twenty, altogether, by the time we had this most recent conversation)—I'd watched in dismay as she made one dramatic, life-changing, even catastrophic mistake after another when it came to men, when it came to love.

When I say *watched in dismay*, I mean that I listened to her stories, empathized, comforted, advised, tsk-tsked, clucked, fretted, sighed, and each time hoped for the best—thought perhaps this time it *would* work out.

When we met she was living with one of her teachers. Soon after, she left him for a dashing young man she met while working on a political campaign. Later she became engaged to a fellow graduate student, broke off the engagement at the last minute, married someone else, left him for one of her own graduate students when she herself became a college professor, married that student, moved to a new city and a new teaching job, had a baby with husband number two, moved to another new city and another new teaching job—to which she brought along a graduate student from the last job to act as nanny to her child, only to discover soon after the move that her second husband, her former student, was sleeping with the nanny, her more recent former student.

By the time she called me, the most recent dust had settled. Her husband had forsworn the nanny. She had decided not to leave him, had decided she was "going to be a grownup, for once." She talked about her marriage—her marriage and what it had been like before this crisis—and what she was beginning to see as a pattern, she said: the kind of men with whom she had always gotten involved, the repetitions, each new relationship seeming to represent a new beginning— something altogether different and vastly improved—and yet now, as she looked back over all of it, an endless succession, she realized, of "the same thing, with enough variations so I could trick myself into thinking it was new, and better." She sighed. "You know how I feel?" she asked.

"Bad?" I said. "Sad? Angry?"

"I feel like a Freudian caricature."

"Ah," I said. "We all are, aren't we, sometimes?"

But now, she went on, she had it covered: plenty of psychotherapy, an understanding at last of what she'd been up to all her life with men—and why—and a determination to break the pattern, as well as to stay in this marriage and make it work. "It's not all about me. It can't be anymore." She was going to put her child's needs first, she said, and she'd concluded that this meant both parents, together, all of them in one house. She was going to *deal*, she said. "Although I've got to tell you, I feel like I'm in the loneliest marriage in the world."

I told her gently that I thought there might be a lot of competition for that title. And that I admired her determination and her sober assessment of the situation, her devotion to the well-being of her child, her willingness to do the "hard thing." I wished her luck, and I meant it.

And then, just before we hung up, she said, "Oh, there's something else I should tell you. One other piece of news — or . . . I don't know, information." And then she told me about the other man — eight years younger than she, a student ("But not *my* student — I know better than that now"), with whom she'd been involved for some time. I didn't ask how long. I didn't ask why. I didn't, in fact, say a thing. I didn't have to, because she was talking very fast, without leaving pauses for responses. "And he really wants me to be with him," she said. "He wants to 'take me away from all this.' This really feels like . . . I don't know, a chance to be happy, finally." She sighed. "So, you know . . . it's hard to know what to do, in the end."

I meant what I told her. Sometimes I think we *are* all "Freudian caricatures." Except that I am not so hard on us as that. I don't think of it as *caricature*. I think of it — of us all — the way I think of characters in novels. Because everything we do has meaning, and just like characters in novels — even the most self-conscious, reflective, wise characters in novels — we so often miss the point: we don't understand ourselves what we're doing, or why, while we're doing it.

This was what Freud had in mind: that we are strangers to ourselves — that we are forever surprising ourselves, misunderstanding ourselves, for all intents and purposes meeting ourselves anew, again and again.

Is it so peculiar to "read" life the way one reads a novel or a poem or *The Wizard of Oz?*

To be honest, I should perhaps admit that I read life *more* closely than I read art. Because I *want* to be lost in the world of a novel — or a piece of music, or a film, or a painting, or a poem. When I read a novel, I fall into it headfirst — so that, indeed, I hated the way I was taught to read in high school and in college: as if there were a code I needed to break in order to understand what I was immersed in. (It is an irony of my life, no doubt, that I teach now in an English department, surrounded by people who read novels in a way that is anathema to me.) So perhaps what I mean to say is not that I read life as I read literature, but that I read life the way I read my dreams — or for that matter my own fiction, in its earliest drafts, when I stand back and wonder over what I've written.

I know the difference between life and art, so it's not as if I'm looking for a grand design in life, or for the sort of unity and structure, *craft*, that a finished work of art exhibits—the big picture. In life, it is impossible to get the big picture. We never have the chance to see our lives all at once, but we can see patterns—and even story arcs, and "through lines." There are metaphors everywhere. And bit by bit, it seems to me, we can make sense of pieces of it. If we look closely enough. And if we keep looking—if we don't stop and say, "There now, *that's* done."

Life itself sometimes seems to me like a dream. The very narrative of daily life will shift sometimes to reflect the symbolic rather than the "real," and these waking symbolic experiences—metamorphosias, phobias, "irrational" responses to situations, "accidents" like the left-behind jacket or slips of the tongue (and for that matter behavior of all kinds: my old friend's romantic adventures; my hovering, overprotective "mothering" during my daughter's childhood)—can be *more* difficult to parse than our dreams are, if only because we don't experience them as dreams; we experience them as "real life," which we so often imagine is not like art at all, and thus has no "meaning."

But there's nothing that happens in life that doesn't strike me as worth looking at for possible meaning, and when something unusual or particularly dramatic occurs, something *apparently* meaningful—the left-behind jacket, Getting-Smaller-and-Getting-Bigger—for me it's only natural, even reflexive, to try to make sense of it, for it seems to me that what we call "symptoms" result from emotions so extreme and insistent they *have* to make their way into "real life," that dreams simply aren't a large enough canvas for the artist that is the unconscious.

My father, who as a child was paid scant attention by his parents—was left to his own devices, reared with no concern for his well-being beyond his most basic physical needs—is guided in his "ordinary" life as in his dream life by an unconscious that must make itself known. His dreams have apparently proved insufficient, and in "real" life he responds with rage to situations in which he is treated as "nothing special" (for example, when he has to wait his turn in a long line). Several years ago, after an evening he endured against his will (he and my mother had come to a reading I gave in Brooklyn at which there were three other writers on the bill, and my mother and I hushed him when he suggested that we all leave after I was finished), not only did he fall into the blackest of moods, refusing to speak to either of us on the way back to Manhattan, but that night he had a dream that shook him so badly he couldn't get out of bed to say goodbye when I left for the airport, to return to Ohio—a first. He had dreamed that he'd killed his father, and woke up in tears.

I have said that I think of us the way I think of characters in novels. Perhaps I should say instead that I think of us as if we were all people in our own dreams.

In dreams, we can't know everything, and we don't expect to. Mysterious, and largely unknowable—only partly knowable—is what a dream is *supposed* to be.

And yet somehow in my determination to understand how the unconscious guides behavior and experience, for a long time I proceeded as if it were possible to know everything. As if—unlike dreams, unlike art—the narratives that make up our lives could provide absolute clarity, perfect matches of cause and effect. As if there might never be moments when we must bow our heads to the mysteries.

As if the unconscious were not, after all, an artist.

In the fever of my search for "answers"—for explication, for mechanisms, a how-to guide to human experience—I made the mistake of thinking of the unconscious as if it were in the business of designing ad campaigns: as if its function were to *persuade* (efficiently, yet always indirectly—"creatively," as they say in advertising). But the unconscious is not *in* business. The unconscious is a poet, working instinctively, and subtly, making choices that have to do with artistic rightness, with grace and unity, beauty, the clarity that has to do with image and meaning and music. And if I don't expect or even desire that a poet—or a painter, or a composer, or a novelist—will explain every choice she has made, explicate the how and why of a work of art, using diagrams to illustrate and clarify all points, why would I expect the unconscious to be able to account for itself?

And if I don't expect or even desire that *we* (the readers, viewers, listeners) should be able to examine a work of art and fully account for it, to successfully analyze the precise relationship between intention and execution and determine how the artist has managed to *get the job done* (and to announce for certain what the job at hand was, as critics so often want to do—as they so often try, and fail, to do), why would I imagine that we might be able to pin down the work of the unconscious in this way?

I know why. It is because the temptation to make the unmanageable manageable is so irresistible. Like my daughter, when she was a child, holding on to anything she had touched, piling up her stuffed animals in the same order every night, matching bumps and knocks and trips—like all of us at one time or another, in one way or another—I thought I might build a fortress against chaos, against the darkness, anxiously denying all the while that a certain amount of chaos, of dark, of *some things just are*, is inescapable, is necessary, is part of human experience itself.

I spent years trying to help my daughter find a balance between the wholehearted engagement with the world of thought and feeling that a full life demands, and the uncertainties, even terror, that such openness—choices, reckonings, a willingness to confront the unknown—might lead to. *Would* lead to. Must, at times, lead to. I tried to teach her that the unknown must be met with a level gaze, that the terror would pass, that acceptance of what can't be planned for, known, categorized, *managed*, is part of the beauty and glory of our lives. But this isn't always easy to do, and I sometimes lose sight of it myself—or close my eyes against it.

To make sense of everything we do, or feel, or see, or *are* is a hopeless undertaking. But just as art is meant to be contemplated, engaged with, speculated about, *felt*—and, inevitably, interpreted—we are surely meant to contemplate the "work" of the unconscious as it reveals itself in each of our lives, and to appreciate its artistry.

Even if we cannot—and perhaps in part because we cannot—fully account for it.

We can only *look*—and see what we will see.

sightline books

The Iowa Series in Literary Nonfiction